I have been long convinced that th
that people can carry with them an
of freedom in the course of the day
such treasure troves of nourishmer
ently suitable for busy people who long for the breath of the
Spirit in the course of a hectic day. A brilliant communicator,
very much in touch with the 'ordinary person', he asks the right
questions and gently directs the readers in searching for the
truth. This book is meant not so much to be read as to be lived
and enjoyed.

✠ *Brendan Comiskey, Bishop Emeritus of Ferns*

Apart from the power of simple articulate utterance, Jack
MacArdle's great strength as a spiritual author is that he wears
his heart on his sleeve. There are many conflicting voices clam-
ouring for our attention in this media-driven world. Very often
the most strident, most cynical wins the day. Here is a voice, as
powerful in its gentleness as it is profound in its simplicity.
Questions I Have Been Asked and Answers I Have Given is an em-
powering resource for those who seek to deepen their understanding of the connection between long established Christian
practices and the incredible love affair between God and his
human children which we call Salvation History.

Pacelli O'Rourke, RE Teacher

Over the years I have benefited greatly from Fr Jack's writings.
He has the knack of expressing the most profound truths in a
language that can be understood by anybody. This latest book is
a gem. It asks and answers many of my own questions, and
questions I have been asked by others. It will be a source of great
inspiration for many, as well as a spiritual guide to those who
need good solid spiritual nourishment. He has met one of my
needs, and for that I will always be grateful.

Carol O'Regan, Pastoral Co-ordinator

Jack McArdle SSCC

Questions

I HAVE BEEN ASKED
AND ANSWERS I HAVE GIVEN

the columba press

First published in 2008 by
the columba press
55A Spruce Avenue, Stillorgan Industrial Park,
Blackrock, Co Dublin

Cover by Bill Bolger
Cover photo by Kevin McLaughlin
Origination by The Columba Press
Printed in Ireland by ColourBooks Ltd, Dublin

ISBN 978 1 85607 599 2

Table of Contents

Dedication

My heartfelt thanks to my sister, Ann Cooper, and her husband Brian,
who watered and fed me, and provided ideal conditions for work
during the writing of this book.
I hope and pray that they share in the blessings
that I myself experienced.

Introduction

Over the years, during my time as a teacher, or Retreat giver, there was always somebody around waiting for an opportunity to pose a question. I liked this, and I took their questions seriously, because I believe that, when it comes to God, I find that I will always have many more questions than answers. Rilke, the philosopher, says that 'Life is a journey from the certainties of callow youth, to a time when I find myself living with questions. I learn to live with the questions, and I even come to love the questions, knowing that, at some future time, I will come into possession of all the answers.' I myself have many more questions now than in my 'callow youth', when I knew all the answers! I encourage people to question their beliefs. While not posing as an answer looking for questions, or a solution looking for problems, I am happy to express an opinion, or to share what I believe. I think it is more important to share what I believe than simply to share what I think.

The questions contained in this book are important ones. I do not believe that the answers are in any way definitive. The best that can be said about them is that they satisfy me ... for now. Probably ten years from now, I could write answers with very different emphases, even if the central tenets remain the same. Certainly, my own understanding of the question will continue to evolve. This is all part of God's revelation. Even in heaven, I don't expect to be able to understand very much about the mystery that is God. Maybe that is why we are given an eternity in order to experience the many facets of the Divinity.

This is not a catechism. As I answered these questions, the readers I had in mind are those who are already involved, and who need reassurance that their understandings and practices are reasonably accurate. I intend these answers to serve as an encouragement to some of those good souls who are led to ask the questions. I hope these answers will serve to confirm those who

are on the Way, and that their own personal experiences will fill
out what is lacking in my answers. From a selfish point of view,
this book has already served a purpose, in so far as I gained
much, and was blessed aplenty in thinking through the answers.
My prayer is for the important added bonus that the reader may
gain much, and be blessed greatly in the reading.

What do you mean when you say 'God is Love'?

The words 'love' and 'God' are interchangeable. 'Love' is the most used and abused word in every language of the world. It is the subject of novels, films, and songs. All of our 'soaps' are saturated with attempts to find love, and the trauma that results from looking for love in the wrong places. Quite frankly, very little of this has anything to do with God. There is such a thing as human love. Because I am human, I am mortal, I will die. Therefore, everything I do on a human level will also die. When we speak about God being love we are speaking of a totally different kind of love altogether. 'In this is love, not that we love God, but that God first loved us' (1 Jn 4:10). 'My dear friends, let us love one another for love comes from God. Everyone who loves is born of God, and knows God ... If such has been the love of God, we, too, must love one another' (1 Jn 4:7, 11). We are invited to stand under the Niagara of the Father's love, which is poured into our hearts. When this happens, this love begins to flow out to those around us. When the love comes from God, the supply is endless, and we will never run short of love to pour out on those around us.

Blessed Mother Teresa could speak with great conviction and excitement around God's love, and that was why she could open both her arms, and say 'Give me all your unwanted babies, and I will take care of them.' She could issue this brave invitation, because she knew that she would have enough love to embrace all those babies. What flows to us from God is poured out on those around us, and thus it is God that is loving others through us. Love is a gift from God, the source of all love, and it becomes the fruit of love when it is poured out upon others. Jesus came across a tree with beautiful leaves, but with no fruit, so he cursed it, and it withered. Love from God that does not go out to others is 'still-born', is barren, and does not bear fruit. The more love we give, the more love we receive. The love I speak of here is so

9

different from human love, that it is not possible for the human mind to grasp the width, the depth, the height, or the extent of it. This is something that we can *experience*, but never understand. Even in heaven, I will never understand the extent of God's love. God-love is the source of all love. On our own, we are like tape-recorders with batteries. We can play, but our life-span is quite limited. However, if we are plugged into the source socket of all love, we will have an endless supply for every moment, situation, and person we meet on the road of life.

The proof that we have this love is shown through a willingness and facility to confirm other people, and make them feel worthwhile. A tendency to 'knock' and to 'put down' others is clear proof that we are not operating with the love of God in our hearts. God's love is always creating, always making all things new. The love that surrounds the new-born baby continues the process of creation in that baby. That baby will grow into a healthy, wholesome, happy human being, if that love continues long after birth. It's fairly easy to be a father, but there's a lot of investment of love that goes in to being a daddy. 'See what singular love the Father has for us; not only are we called children of God, but we really are' (Jn 3:1).

'The saint is not the person who loves God, but the person who is convinced that God loves her' (Van Breeman, *As Bread That Is Broken*). In this same book, faith is defined as *the courage to accept God's acceptance*. At the moment of death I will stand before God exactly as I am. No more hiding, excusing, denying, or blaming. I can do that now, every moment of every day. I can open out the canvas of my life before him, knowing that he sees *all* that is there anyhow, so there's not much point in coming to him in any other way. To know that God loves me is a *gift*. That is what Jesus means when he says 'No one knows the Father except the Son, and those to whom the Son chooses to reveal him' (Lk 10:22). 'Jesus, please reveal the Father's love to me' is a lovely prayer that we could make our own.

If there could be unhappiness in heaven, it would surely come from seeing all those people longing to be loved, yearning for love, and looking and searching for love in all the wrong places. This often leads to great hurts, much abuse and rejection, and many tears. Of course, from the perspective of heaven, it must be obvious just how weak, fragile, and vulnerable we really are. I'm sure there are prayers said for us in heaven, and I know those prayers must surely help. However, not all the prayers of heaven and earth can take away our right to exercise our free-will. Jesus didn't want Judas to go out and hang himself, but he couldn't stop him. Jesus cried many bitter tears as he overlooked his beloved Jerusalem. He so much wanted to help them, and bring them under the Father's love, but they refused to accept all his offers. 'How often have I tried to bring together your children, as a hen gathers her young under her wings, but you would not' (Lk 13:34). Love is essentially unconditional, and there can never be conditions or price tags attached. When I buy a gift for someone, the first thing I do is to remove the price tag, or ask the shop assistant to do that for me. Genuine love is freely given, and freely received. That is why there can be no love without free-will. Without free-will there can be no relationships, there can be no good. Without free-will, I am deprived of all other options; therefore, what I do has no moral value, because I am nothing better than a robot that is programmed to perform in a predetermined and non-optional way. Free-will is an extraordinary gift, even though it may frighten us at times.

Not many parents could say to their children 'You can do whatever you like, and I'll still love you.' Most of us would be afraid to give another a *carte blanche* to do whatever he or she wants to do. If it were within our power, we would probably remove all those occasions, things, and people that might lead our friend into wrong-doing. They would end up being 'conned' into being good people!

This helps us to realise that our love can be riddled with fear. We can even claim to love God, and genuinely want to do so, and yet have that element of fear. 'There is no fear in love. Perfect love drives out fear, for fear has to do with punishment; they who fear do not know perfect love' (1 Jn 4:18). In this we see the connectedness between love and trust. That is what was meant in a sentence quoted earlier 'Faith is to have the courage to accept the acceptance of God.'

I had a funeral recently of an elderly lady in a nursing home where I minister. During the days of the funeral, there were many times when I heard it said about Kathleen 'She was a beautiful lady, and she always saw the best in everyone.' Her ability to see the best in everyone was intended and accepted as a genuine tribute to her own goodness. When God created, he looked, and 'He saw that it was good'. When he looks at us now, he still sees that we are good, as shown by the forgiving father rushing out, with open arms, to welcome and embrace his Prodigal Son. To have the courage to stand beneath the Niagara of the Father's love is to come to experience the forgiveness of God, and to grow into an experiential knowledge of the Father's love.

I can have a certain feeling of being forgiven; I can know that I am forgiven. When I was a child I had a dog that looked really guilty whenever he did something wrong, like chasing the postman, or stealing something from the kitchen table. He lay on his back, expecting a smack or a scolding. If I patted him in a friendly way, he would bound up, and jump all over me! He knew he was forgiven. What will complete my experience of being forgiven is when I learn to apply that forgiveness to myself. To stand under the Niagara of the Father's love is to be washed of all guilt.

Jesus asks us to love one another (and ourselves) as he loves us. 'Neither do I condemn you.' You should look in a mirror sometime and say that to yourself. Part of God's forgiveness of you must surely include the grace to be able to forgive yourself. I imagine that when Jesus healed the leper he healed the *whole* person. If the leper went down the road filled with resentment towards his brother, it could hardly be said that he was healed. If you do not forgive yourself, then it can truly be said that you are not forgiven. If you are convinced that God loves you, and has forgiven you, then surely you must accept the need to forgive yourself. We say to Jesus 'By your cross and resurrection you have set us free.' What a pity, then, if we fail to set ourselves free! 'In him there is no condemnation' says Paul. Paul also tells us that we no longer are slaves, but we can come without fear into the presence of God, calling God 'Abba, Father.'

I want to repeat something from earlier because I think it needs to be repeated again and again. When God forgives, he suffers from total amnesia. Not only does he remove the sin, but he can actually heal all the evil effects of that sin. He can remove the guilt, the regret, the self-condemnation, and the shame. I can look back, and acknowledge the sin, but it remains 'back there', and none of the guilt, shame, or regret comes back with that moment of recall. The only value the past has are the lessons it taught me. Any compassion I have in my life has come from my own brokenness and failures. The Lord can turn my failures into grace, and even those failures can be turned into good. 'For those who love God, all things work together onto good.' I couldn't imagine Jesus healing somebody, and letting him go on down the road full of bitterness towards his brother. I believe that Jesus heals the total person, or not at all.

The question posed was 'What do you mean when you say that "God is Love"?' My attempt at an answer is saying that God is the *source of all love*, and when we speak of love it should/ could be written in capital letters. All human love is but a pale reflection of that *love*. Speaking of this kind of love, Paul says that 'Love is patient, kind, without envy. It is not boastful or arrogant. It is not ill-mannered, nor does it seek its own interest. Love overcomes anger, and forgets offences. It does not take delight in wrong, but rejoices in truth. Love excuses everything, believes all things, hopes all things, endures all things. Love will never end … Now we have faith, hope, and love, but the greatest of these is *love*' (1 Cor 13:4-8, 13).

When we die, we will no longer need faith or hope, because we will be living with everything we believed in, and everything we hoped for. We will, however, always need love. Surely Paul is speaking of God's love here, because I don't think many of us could claim to have such love in us. However, we can live with the sure and certain hope that God will fill us with this wonderful gift when we are ready to receive and exercise it. My generation grew up with what I might call 'An Old Testament God' ... a fire-and-thunder God, who threatened scourges and floods on those who fell foul of him, and who was very much into law and obedience. God was someone to be feared, rather than loved. We had long lists of sins, and catalogues of graces, merits, and indulgences. Guilt was the order of the day, and death was something that only the most spiritual people welcomed. The emphasis was on religion, rather than spirituality. Religion is external; it is what *we* do. It is about rules and regulations, and it is about *control*. Spirituality, on the other hand, is internal; it is about what God does, and it is about *surrender*. Jesus died to bring people across a bridge from the love of law to the law of love, from religion to spirituality. Religion, divorced from spirituality, has always been a source of destruction. There is not a war in today's world that is not caused by religion.

When I came along all those years later, the church had gone back over that bridge again into the love of law. Blessed John XXIII, of happy memory, before launching Vatican II, prayed out to God for 'a new Pentecost of love and understanding' ... hoping to bring the church back over the bridge again. I believe that we did receive a New Pentecost, and we are now living in the Acts of the Apostles of that Second Pentecost. Among much evidence of that, which will come up in a later answer, I point to the fact that Pope Benedict XVI wrote a letter, shortly after his election, and, guess what it is called? 'God is Love.' He now has published the first ten chapters of a new book, and that is going to be my kick-off point in answering the next question.

P.S. These are *exciting times*! Praise God!

What do the gospels tell us about God?

Yes, indeed, Pope Benedict XVI is my starting point for this answer. He has just written a book, which is now available in English. It is entitled *Jesus of Nazareth*. It is an unusual book … surprise! surprise! … in that he does his writing in his spare time, of which he has very little. Being a humble man, and a very practical man, he announced some time ago that he had completed the first ten chapters of his book, and he was going to publish them now. He said if the Lord gave him enough time and enough health, he would finish the book sometime, and the rest of the book would be published later. Judging by the size (and the weight!) of the first ten chapters, the completed work will probably run into three volumes.

The above question asks 'What do the gospels tell us about God?' Pope Benedict tells us that *the gospels are all about God*. Jesus told us that 'they who see me see the Father. They who hear me hear the Father. The Father and I are one' (Jn 14:9). What Pope Benedict emphasises is that, when we watch Jesus in action in the gospels, we are *watching God*. Most believers accept that Jesus is God, but one gets the feeling sometimes that he's not considered to be the 'whole thing'! Some of us hold on to our image of that hoary old Man in the sky, with the long flowing beard, who is watching us, writing down everything we do and say, and will demand a strict and rigid account of our every word and act when we come before him in death. We can accept that Jesus is 'very nice', but then 'there's this other God …'

The blame for this can hardly be laid at the feet of Jesus!.He was clear and unambiguous about his mission. 'I never say anything unless the Father tells me.' 'My meat is to do the will of him who sent me.' Our own confusion and lack of clarity regarding this whole question comes from the theologians' distinction between what they call the 'Jesus of History' and the 'Christ of Faith'. It can appear as if there were two Persons involved! Without getting too 'bogged down' in theological jargon and concepts, let me make the following distinction. The 'Jesus of History' refers to the Jesus who walked the roads of Galilee, who was born and died there. The 'Christ of Faith' could be understood as the corpus of his teaching, and all that he left for us to believe, to teach, and to act on, after he returned to his Father. In other words, it was a system of teachings and beliefs rather than a real Person. The 'Jesus of History' was down-to-earth, and we could relate to him, but the Christ of Faith became some sort of mythologised Person, with whom it was difficult to have a *real* relationship. Christianity is not about producing nicer people with better morals. I could be a pagan, and be all of that. Neither is it about prayer and fasting. I could be a Muslim and do all of that. Christianity is about a *person*, Jesus Christ. The Messenger is the Message.

What Pope Benedict is saying, and what this answer will attempt to present, is that when you look at Jesus, you are looking at God. That is God who goes down into the Jordan river, among all the sinners, in order to be baptised by John the Baptist. That is God who goes into the desert to be tempted by Satan. This knowledge can be both a source of happiness and of puzzlement for us at the same time. We are happy to get such a close-up view of God, yet we can be puzzled that God allowed Satan to tempt and to bully him. In a later scene in the gospel, Jesus is asked why a particular man was born blind. Was it because of his own sins, or the sins of his fathers? Jesus told them it was neither, but it was that the glory of God might be seen in his healing. That is why God (Jesus) allowed himself to be tempted, so that Satan's powerlessness over him could be displayed. Thus it was in humbling himself that Jesus was exalted. The next time you read this story about the temptations in the desert, just remind yourself that this is *God* being tempted. The same reminder is necessary when reading any and every other incident in the gospels.

Look at Jesus with the children. That is God who is playing with them. He threw back his head and laughed. He pulled funny faces, and pretended he was hiding, as he put his hands over his face, and peeped through his fingers at them. Any parent will tell you that a child will never go near anybody who doesn't laugh, and pull funny faces … and make them laugh. That is God you are looking at in that scene.

Lepers were labelled 'unclean'; they had to keep their distance, and no one was supposed to go near them, because of the fear of infection that prevailed at that time. Watch Jesus standing to listen to, and speak to the leper, and then reaching out to touch him. That is God you are watching. Think about that in the context of the last question about God being love. The gospels record many encounters with lepers, but I'm sure that this was a regular occurrence. One of the priests in my own Congregation (Blessed Damien of Molokai) went to work among the lepers. He spent the first few weeks there out under the bushes in the open, because the stench made it impossible for him to enter a house. Eventually, he was sitting in their houses, sharing his pipe with them, eating meal out of the same bowl as them (who tried to retain a fist of meal despite their missing fingers). He bathed, bandaged, and buried them. The love of the Father that was poured out upon him soon began to flow out to them. And once again, we need to be reminded that this was God in action.

God has no grandchildren; we are all children of God. That is why Jesus treated Jew, Samaritan, or Roman with equal respect and reverence. That is God speaking to the woman at the well. It was as if God said 'These people don't understand me. They don't know how I want them to love each other, so I'll go down myself and show them.' The Acts of the Apostles begin with these words: 'In the first part of my work, I wrote of all that Jesus *did and taught* from the beginning, until the day when he ascended into heaven' (Acts 1:1). Notice that Jesus *did* the action first, and then he *taught* his disciples how to do that. He washed their feet before asking them to wash one another's feet. I called to a convent some time ago, and was moved to see a very symbolic set-up just inside the front door. It was an earthen-ware jug of water sitting in an earthen-ware basin, with a large towel

draped over the lot. It symbolised a welcome for the weary san-
daled traveller who had trekked through the desert to reach this
door. No marks for guessing what all that recalled to me.

To understand Jesus' treatment of women, one has to understand the norms of that time. The gospel tells us that Jesus fed
five thousand men, 'not counting women and children'. The
words 'not counting' are significant. The gospels are replete
with stories, anecdotes, and incidents where Jesus encountered
women whom he treated with the greatest respect. Those he
found that were down-trodden and marginalised, he raised up
and gave them dignity. The list is endless, but it is worth more
than just a passing reference. From Elizabeth to Anna in the
Temple, from the widow of Naim to the woman who touched
the hem of his garment; from the prostitute washing his feet to
the one he rescued from being stoned to death; the list goes on
and on. It is significant, however, that women outnumbered the
men on Calvary, and they were the first people to be told about
the resurrection. Once again, when we witness Jesus' encounter
with the women, we have to remind ourselves that this is God in
action. Even in today's world, with all our advances in civilis-
ation and expertise, we need to look again at how God treated
women in the gospels. There is not one religion on this earth that
can claim to be an equal-opportunity haven for women, where
they are given the same rights as men. In Jesus, God could have
come among us in an instant in one of any and all possible ways,
but he chose to identify himself with us by being born of a
woman. In doing this, he raised the status of women to a unique
and sacred place. It is significant that Jesus' mother holds such a
place of honour and reverence in the Christian story, followed
by a special place of honour in Islam.

Looking closer at the encounters Jesus had with the two prostitutes, or 'public sinners', as they were called, gives us a
glimpse of God's love in a very special way. The story of the
woman who came to Jesus while he was in the house of a
Pharisee makes for riveting reading. While in the company of
Pharisees, Jesus knew that his every movement was monitored,

THE GOSPELS AND GOD

and he was in the lens of the tabloid cameras at all times. They searched for every excuse to use against him. I'm sure the air was 'stuffy', and the atmosphere was tense. I doubt if the invitation was motivated by love, reverence, or loyalty. Almost on cue this public sinner walked in. A hush fell on whatever conversation there was, and all eyes were riveted on Jesus' face. Under normal circumstances, the woman would not have got past the front door. For the Pharisees, however, this was an extraordinary gifted opportunity, rather than the problem it would have presented in different circumstances. This woman was, literally, putting her life on the line, her head on the block. She followed some inner instinct that made her immune to the sneers that surrounded her, and she walked straight to Jesus, and knelt at his feet. Not a word was spoken as she sobbed, and the tears fell directly onto the feet of Jesus. One by one, she took each foot and washed it with those tears. Without a thought, she let her long hair fall over the feet, and she used that hair to dry the tears away. What a golden opportunity for a Pharisee who sought each and every opportunity to undermine Jesus, and his message. The look in Jesus' eyes was enough to confirm their worst convictions. He looked on the woman with a tender look of love and compassion. This was not a 'show' for Jesus, or the woman, even though it was the best show in town for those who looked on. Jesus then spoke, and he spoke quietly, with reverence and conviction. His words were simple, but very powerful. This woman loved him, and she showed her love, and he felt that he was loved. He compared her expression of love to the cold and formal welcome of his host, and he told them that she could not love like that and be alienated from God at the same time. 'Her sins, her many sins, are forgiven her, because she loved so much.'

That was the final nail in his coffin, as far as his listeners were concerned. Once again, let us remember that this is *God in action*. It is a close-up vignette of an encounter between God and a sinner. All the on-lookers were sinners also, of course, but it was the disposition or attitude of this woman that made all the difference. Any of those who looked on could just as surely have received the same look of love from Jesus, but they rejected that. Each had his own agenda and, compared to the woman, they marched to the beat of a different drum.

The encounter with the woman condemned to death by stoning has so many similar characteristics to the one on which we have just reflected that there is no need to deal with it at any great length. Suffice it to say that this was yet another opportunity that both the Pharisees and Jesus welcomed, but for very different reasons. They were all set to attack the woman with stones, until Jesus gently but firmly turned the attack on them with truth. His truth unarmed and neutered them straightaway, and they had no option but to slip away quietly. Jesus was left alone with the woman. He spoke to her with a voice that was neither condescending nor demeaning. 'Has anyone condemned you?' 'No one, sir', she answered. 'Well neither do I condemn you. Go in peace.' I sometimes wonder if either woman lived long enough to discover that it was God each had encountered on each of those days. I sometimes fantasise meeting them in heaven, and listening to their memories of how each felt on those occasions.

Jesus was a teacher rather than a preacher. The preacher tells us what to do, the teacher shows us how to do it. Like any good teacher, Jesus used stories, anecdotes, and parables to help get his message across. The most powerful story in the gospels is the story of the Prodigal Son. This is a classic, and it aptly summarises the central message of the gospels. 'The Father sent me to invite you back to the Garden, where a big hug awaits you', would be a summary of that message. This story gives us a view of the Father up close. 'I never say anything unless the Father tells me' says Jesus. Obviously, the Father told him to tell us this story. We need look no further beyond this story to get a clear understanding of the love of the Father. The question under consideration is about what the gospels tell us about God. The answer to that question is summarised in this story. It is called the Story of the Prodigal Son, but it could be called the Story of the Forgiving

Father. It contains *all* the elements of unconditional love, from generosity to trust to forgiveness to compassion. It makes no demands whatsoever, and it lays down no conditions. It displays forgiveness of a very high level. No wonder we say 'To err is human; to forgive is divine.'

When we examine the story we get a better idea of how deep was the rejection that the father received from his son. It wasn't just a question of squandering and wasting money. To do what he did meant squandering his upbringing, rejecting all that his family stood for, and seriously jeopardising his future. The son could not have sunk any lower, yet the father's love and concern for him could not have been any higher. It takes love that could only be divine to bridge such a vast chasm. No lectures, no scolding, no penance. The father met him with a smothering hug. His son was dirty, smelly, and in rags, yet the father clasped him to his chest, and held him firmly, until the son was sure that the forgiveness was real. Remember, in the story, the son did not come home for this, and did not expect it. He came home to offer himself as one of his father's servants. It must have been the overpowering emotion of the father's love that rekindled the fire of hope within that young man's heart. In some extraordinary way, he just knew that he was forgiven. He may not have fully understood the dynamics of it, but he felt certain that he was forgiven. The feast, and all that went with it, confirmed that feeling. He was deeply affected when his father ordered sandals for him, because sandals were worn only by people who were travelling. In other words, the father was removing all conditions and, if the son chose to wander off again, he was free to do so.

Pope Benedict speaks of all that Jesus brought to us, e.g. his teaching, his love, his forgiveness, and a whole new hope. He summarises all of that by stressing that Jesus brought *God* to us. 'The Kingdom of God is among you.' Jesus had brought God into each and every situation. I will finish off here, because I don't think we need further evidence of what the gospels tell us about God. The gospels *are* about God!

How important is Pentecost?

Pentecost is the *pinnacle* of the church calendar. All things are restored in Pentecost. When the mission of Jesus was complete, he returned to the Father, and he sent the Holy Spirit to complete his work on earth, and to bring us the fullness of grace. Jesus always had the Spirit within him, because he was united to the Father and the Spirit in the unbreakable bond of the Trinity.

However, to clearly demonstrate the role of the Spirit, Jesus joined the sinners at the Jordan river and, for the edification of the onlookers, the Spirit was seen to come upon him. When he came up out of the waters, he headed for the desert for his first battle with Satan, and he then proceeded to launch his mission. His words and his actions were accompanied by signs and wonders, and his followers marvelled at the power that was given him. Towards the end of his mission, he told his disciples that they, too, would receive that Spirit, and 'greater things than this will you do'. In other words, the Spirit would do in and through us, what he did in and through Jesus. When the apostles realised that Jesus was about to leave them, they were sad, but Jesus told them that it was better for them that he go, because if he did not go the Holy Spirit would not come. If he did go, he would send the Spirit to them, and that Spirit would never leave them. Important and all as his presence with them was, he told them that it was more important that the Spirit should come than that he should stay with them.

That is quite a significant phrase. The Father initiated the process. Jesus launched the work of salvation, and overcame the obstacles on the road to salvation. Now the Spirit would come to guide us, and to inspire us on our journey back to the Garden. When Jesus returned to his Father, the work of redemption was done, but our response to that was only beginning. It is the work of the Spirit to provide this final part of the jigsaw.

The apostles lived with Jesus for three years. They listened to him, watched him, and spoke to him. They saw him raise the dead, calm the storms, and cleanse the lepers. At the end of it all, however, once the pressure came, they denied him, sold him, and deserted him. They had not changed. They needed something more than the example of Jesus' life and teachings. They needed what he had, and that would require the Spirit coming in person upon each one of them. Jesus rose from the dead on Easter Sunday, but nothing happened to anyone else. That evening they would have sold, denied, and deserted him all over again, if the pressure returned. They needed something, and that something was the Holy Spirit.

Pentecost for them paralleled the Annunciation for Mary, and both words are interchangeable. They would have to surrender, say their own *Fiat*, and agree to be led by the Spirit. Mary was given responsibility for their preparation for this event. She had travelled this road before them, and was fully conscious of how this promise would be fulfilled.

If I had the ability to write drama, I would love to put on paper what I imagine happened in that Upper Room during those nine days (Novena), as they waited for the Spirit to come. Peter grew impatient as the days passed by, with nothing happening, and he wanted to go home. Thomas was doubtful, and believed less and less in the promise as time went by. I imagine that, without the presence of Mary, they would not have remained there for the nine days. Elizabeth said to Mary, 'All these things happened to you because you believed that the promises of the Lord would be fulfilled.' The Spirit came because he was expected to come. Mary never doubted that Jesus would keep his promise, and so, no matter how long she had to wait, she was not leaving till the Spirit came. For the apostles everything was changed, changed utterly. Nothing in their lives would ever be the same again. Just as the stone had been rolled away from the tomb, as Jesus emerged into New Life, so the doors of the Upper Room were flung open, and the apostles came forth with fire in their bellies, as men with a mission.

The question is 'How important is Pentecost?' The answer,

simply, is 'If Pentecost had not happened, the whole mission of Jesus would be a failure; it would be incomplete, unfinished.' It is important, indeed vital, that we apply that answer to ourselves.

Let me put it this way. Many Christians get off the train too soon. We travel with Jesus from Christmas to Ash Wednesday, through Lent, Holy Week, Good Friday to Easter. The temptation is to get off the train at Easter, to wave the banners, and to proclaim 'Alleluia! Alleluia! He is risen from the dead!' The problem with this is that the terminus is Pentecost, and we got off the train too soon! Jesus told his apostles to stay in Jerusalem until the Spirit came (don't get off the train!). If they left too soon, it was entirely predictable how they would end up. *This is vital*. All of what went before (Christmas, Easter, etc.) has come to *nothing* if we don't wait for Pentecost. *Every Christian must have a Pentecost*. How can I possibly stress this enough? This is something that I want to proclaim from the house-tops. It is a message that every Christian *needs* to hear very clearly. In an ideal world, the local parish would gather in the Upper Room on Ascension Thursday, and spend the next nine days in prayer, and be determined not to leave there until the Spirit came. Wow! What a difference that would make in the church!

What happened that first Pentecost is that the church was born. Jesus was incarnated in a different guise, with you and me being members of his Body. A spirit (big or small 's') cannot do anything. An evil spirit needs somebody's hand to plant the bomb, or somebody's tongue to tell the lie. It is the same with the Holy Spirit. During his earthly life, Jesus used the body he received through his mother Mary. In this new life, the only body Jesus has is ours. 'Christ has no body now but yours. No hands, no feet, no voice on earth but yours.' My role is to provide the body. I am not asked or expected to heal anybody, but I am asked to provide the hands to be laid on the sick, so that the Spirit can work through me. When I stand up to preach, I am providing the voice, and expecting the Spirit to do the rest (the part that matters). 'When you stand up to speak on my behalf, don't worry what you shall say. The Spirit will give you words that nobody will be able to contradict.' I do not have to give power to what I do or say. That is the work of the Spirit. Without the Spirit, I am only saying words when I pray. It is the Spirit who turns my words into prayer. I 'tune into' the Spirit before I pray, preach, switch on a computer, pick up a phone, or ring a doorbell. In the words of St Paul I learn to 'live and to walk in the Spirit'. I conducted a Retreat recently, and the organisers, who know me quite well, chose as the theme 'Just Show Up'. Bring the body, and the Spirit will provide everything else. A moment's reflection should help me realise the ratio between the body, which is mine, and the Spirit, which is of God. I might be able to describe it as 'Infinity to one'. If I could become convinced of this truth, my whole life would become like a resurrected life. I could 'ride the wind', like a seagull, and encounter every problem as an opportunity to experience the power of God's Spirit to guide my feet into the way of peace.

We are guided by the Spirit of Truth, who will lead me into all truth … 'and the truth will set you free'. I have reflected at great length on this whole question of Pentecost, because I am not convinced that it is necessarily part of every Christian's life. One of the problems seems to be a lack of clarity between 'having the Spirit', and allowing the Spirit 'have me'. Of course, I have the Holy Spirit, as a result of my baptism. Presuming that my baptism was when I was an infant, then I also had the gift of speech, and of mobility back then. However, I must confess that it required constant and tireless ongoing effort to develop those gifts, and to become agile in both tongue and limbs. Of course, I had the gift of speech and the gift of mobility, but if I had not made constant use of those gifts, until they grew and developed into personal ownership, I would now be backward and disabled in those areas. What I'm trying to say is that I may have the Holy Spirit, but the Holy Spirit may not have me!

All the doors to my heart, soul, and mind are equipped with handles on the inside only. Unless I am ready and willing to hand over the keys of my goodwill, and allow the Spirit have free access, then there will be no Pentecost for me.

Once again, I repeat the question 'How important is Pentecost?', and once again I repeat that without Pentecost, it would be as if Jesus had never come. All that he did, including his death and resurrection, would have been in vain.

How I long for the day when all life in my parish comes to a stop on Ascension Thursday, and we are all invited into the Upper Room for the following nine days. I repeat that I cannot over-stress the centrality of this. This is like our Finals. If we fail this, we fail the whole course, and that life we longed for can never be ours. There is nothing magic or mysterious about this. It is just a question of wanting, of longing, of asking. 'The Father will surely give the Holy Spirit to those who ask.' Every promise of Jesus, regarding the Holy Spirit, is sure and certain, without a 'maybe', a 'might', or 'perhaps' in the whole lot. When Jesus spoke to the Samaritan woman at the well, he spoke to her of a thirst that cannot be quenched by water. There is a thirst within the human spirit that can only be quenched by the Spirit of God. The Spirit is like water breaking through the hard crust of the desert sand, which forms a life-giving oasis for all that pass by. Without the Spirit, there can only be sand.

Many years ago, I was giving a Retreat to a community of Sisters. I was speaking of the Holy Spirit as I have been writing in this chapter. I was in the parlour afterwards having a cup of tea, when there was a knock on the door. A little nun entered, whom I knew to be 93 years of age. She looked at me with the look of an excited and very curious child, as she said 'Father, whatever it is you're talking about, I want it, I want it all, and I want it *now*'! I'm not sure if I spilled my tea, but her words brought me to my feet instantly. I took her by the arm, saying 'Come on, Sister. Let us go down to the Prayer Room and say those words to Jesus. I'm sure he hasn't heard a prayer like that for quite a while!' We went down to the Prayer Room, and she blurted out 'Jesus, whatever it is you're talking about, I want it, I want it all, and I want it now'. I placed my hands on her head, and prayed with her. I could almost hear the shell cracking, as she began to sob, and to shake. It was as if the caterpillar was

26

breaking out of the cocoon and becoming a butterfly. Words of praise and thanks just flowed from her mouth (or from her heart). The following morning, she told me that she had been laughing and crying all night! Two days later, at the closing Mass of the Retreat, when the Sisters were sharing some Prayers of the Faithful, Sister prayed 'Now, Lord, you can dismiss your servant in peace, because my eyes have seen your salvation.' She died in her sleep ten days later. What a wonderful 'conversion' in the final days of her life.

There is a marvellous scene in chapter 37 of the prophet Ezekiel. 'By his Spirit he brought me out, and set me in the middle of a valley which was full of dry bones.' This was how God saw his people, the people of Israel. They considered themselves alive and well but, in the eyes of God, they were withered and dead. The prophet wondered if these people could ever live again, and he asked God about that possibility. God instructed him to speak to the dry bones, and to call on them to come together. Suddenly, there was a loud noise all across the valley, as the bones came together, and formed human bodies, which were soon covered with flesh and skin. However, they were still dead; there was no life in them. The prophet looked to God for his next instructions, and he was told to call on the wind to enter those bodies, like a spirit of life, like the breath that God breathed into the clay at creation. Suddenly, all the bodies came alive, 'standing on their feet … a great, immense army.' God spoke again to the prophet: 'These bones are all Israel. They keep saying "Our bones are dry. All hope is gone. It is the end of us." Say to them "Oh, my people, I am going to open your tombs … and when I open your graves and bring you out of your graves, I will put my Spirit in you, and you shall live".'

There are times when, at a glance, the church resembles that valley of dry bones. It is imperative, it is essential that Pentecost be given the priority and the urgency that it requires. Without Pentecost there is no church. I can take a collection of precious diamonds, and lay them out one by one in a museum. Or I can take them, and make a necklace with them, where they will all complete and enhance each other. The Spirit is given to the church, not to the individual. To the extent that I am a committed member of the Body, am I open to receive the power of that Spirit. When Pope John XXIII looked at the church of his day, he asked the Lord for a New Pentecost. In doing so, he summarised exactly what the church needed. Pentecost is an on-going process of renewal, 'until Christ be formed in you'.

We speak of the body provided to Jesus through the obedience of Mary. Our vocation is exactly like hers. We are asked to provide the body, so that the Spirit can complete the work of Jesus through us. In Eucharistic Prayer IV there is a wonderful statement which goes to the core of the reality: 'That we might live no longer for ourselves, but for him, he sent the Holy Spirit, as his first gift to those who believe, to complete his work in us, and to bring us the fullness of grace.' I rest my case!

How is the Mass connected to Calvary?

Adam and Eve had refused to do what God asked of them. Their sin was one of disobedience. They would do things *their way*, as if they knew better than God, which, of course, was also a sin of pride. The perfect antibiotic or antibody for such a sin, of course, is humble obedience. 'Christ, in the days of his mortal life, offered his sacrifice of tears and cries. He prayed to him who could save him from death, and he was heard because of his humble obedience. Although he was son, he learned through obedience what suffering was and, once made perfect, he became the source of eternal salvation to those who obey him' (Heb 5:7-9).

Calvary was the perfect and complete antidote for the sin of the Garden. On Calvary, Jesus submitted himself totally to the will of the Father, 'even onto death, death on a cross'. On him was pinned all those death-emitting weaknesses we had inherited through Original Sin. They would be nailed to the cross with him and, once he rose from the dead, all those evils had been neutered, had been defused. In the Preface for Easter we say 'The long reign of sin is ended, the whole world has been made new, and we are once again made whole.'

'Dying you destroyed our death.' I stand beside Mary on Calvary, and she stands beside me at the altar when I celebrate Eucharist. Jesus dies only once, but the '*yes*' of that death can be repeated again and again, just as any one of us must repeat a new 'yes' with the dawning of each new day. When I offer Eucharist, I am repeating that 'yes' of Jesus on Calvary, except that I am joining to that my own 'yes' to Jesus now. The chalice represents death for Jesus. 'Father, if it's possible, let this chalice pass from me.' Before holding up the chalice at the Offertory, I place a drop of water in the wine. That is my 'yes' to Jesus, which I am joining to his 'yes' to the Father.

My 'yes' was said for me, as they poured water on me at my baptism. However, as I grow into maturity, I take greater responsibility for my life, and I bring that water back to church, one drop at a time. With it I join my 'yes' to Jesus' 'yes' to the Father.

A Christian is someone who does her dying during her lifetime. Death is like a pile of sand at the end of my life, which I can take and sprinkle, one day at a time, as I travel along the road. I die to my possessions, my opinions, my tiredness, or my pride, in the process of loving others. 'Greater love than this no one has than a person should lay down his life for a friend.' When was the last time you died for another? That was the last time you loved someone. If you wait till the end of your life to die it could be too late. What a privilege it is for us who were not on Calvary!

We can still join in that 'yes', just as if we stood there beside Mary. In the Mass we have a reversal of roles, as if we are shown the other side of the same coin. I was not with Mary on Calvary, but she stands with me at the altar. It is exactly as if it was arranged that I could fully catch up on all that I missed. When I stand at the altar this morning, it is exactly as if I were standing on Calvary on Good Friday. As I stand there on Calvary I can witness love as never before. I hear the words addressed to Mary, to John, to the man on the other cross, to the Father. I see the centurion strike his breast; I see and hear the thunder of the clouds and the earthquakes. I see the dead rising out of their graves, and I *know* this is a *momentous* and *awesome* occasion. When I stand at the altar, I can have a sense of the awesomeness of this place and of this occasion. As I pray, I join Jesus in the role of mediator between God and his people. I hold up that host, just as his body was raised up on Calvary. This is an extraordinary contact moment between the Creator and his creatures, between the Forgiving Father and his prodigal children. 'Heavenly Father, I offer you the body and blood, soul and divinity, of your dearly beloved Son, our Lord Jesus Christ, in atonement for our sins, and the sins of the whole world … For the sake of his sorrowful Passion, have mercy on us and on the whole world.'

Celebrating Eucharist is to *re-enact* the '*yes*' of Calvary. As I said earlier, Jesus dies only once, but the *prayer* that Calvary was can be repeated until the end of time, and the last one will be just as powerful as that first one.

Process is a very important word when it comes to considering the way the Lord works. It is as if the whole lot was based on some sort of gestation process, something that is on-going, and is never complete. Chesterton says that we never *become* Christian; we are always in *the process of becoming*. God's creation of the new baby continues long after birth, as the parents' love continues to incubate it on its journey to maturity. What happened on Calvary continues to echo down the years, and the 'fall-out' from that is on-going. Paul speaks about Christ being formed in us. It is a slow on-going process, and is never really complete until I join him in heaven. It is only then that I will become all that God created me to be. If I eat a slice of bread, that bread becomes part of me, and if I cut a finger, that blood had its source in the food that I ate. When I receive the Bread of Life in Eucharist, the very opposite process happens. I am transformed more and more into what I receive.

On a human level, Calvary was a total disaster, and when I hear people express concerns over the church today, I suspect that they would not have been very happy on Calvary. If I had been on Calvary, the only hope I would have had would have been to stick very close to Mary, and hear her assure me that Easter was only around the corner. The only real sin I can commit, as a Christian, is not to have hope.

I am concerned at times about the lack of understanding and appreciation that many people seem to have about the Mass. It is reasonable to assume that this comes from a lack of proper instruction, formation, and teaching about the meaning and importance of the Mass. I don't honestly believe that people who are brought to a deep personal appreciation of the extraordinary nature of this gift can end up discarding it lightly, or just take it and leave it as they please. The church may be sacramentalising, and the schools may be catechising, but if there is no one evangelising, we end up producing vast hordes of spiritual illiterates. If I am not engaged in evangelising of some kind or other, it is proof positive that I myself have never been evangelised. Not that we are all called to be evangelists, because this is a gift that is not given to everybody. However, we can all give witness, and, in the words of St Peter, we can 'always have an explanation to give to those who ask us the reason for the hope that we have' (1 Pet 3:15). If the teachers of the church are failing to convey to people a deep conviction about the centrality and the extraordinary gift that is Eucharist, then, alas, they are failing miserably, and the mission committed to us by Jesus is being neglected. The problem here may be that the teachers themselves are not really convinced and convicted, and that makes the picture sadder still. People are voting with their feet, and are walking in droves in the other direction when the priest comes out on the altar to offer Eucharist. Jesus experienced that same desertion as he hung on Calvary, with only one of his apostles in sight. Do you think that if they had Mary's conviction, and depth of faith, they would have deserted him? I don't wish to enter into the blame game here, but I do honestly want to investigate why things are as they are relative to attendance at Mass. I have been at some celebrations, and I wasn't convinced that the celebrant was very excited about being up there at the altar, nor did he seem to care too much that I was down in the pew.

We are a Eucharistic people. We are most truly church when we gather around the table of the Lord. I cannot think of any better preparation for entering into the fullness of life than to share in the 'food for the journey' that is provided for us in Eucharist. 'They who eat my Body, and drink my Blood *have* everlasting life, and I *will* raise them up on the Last Day.' All I will have to say, in a later chapter, about prayer being a *gift*, applies especially here. Developing a love and appreciation of Eucharist is one of the special gifts of the Spirit.

The question concerns the connection between Calvary and Eucharist. Mass is the knock-on effect of Calvary, it is Calvary reverberating down the centuries. It is believed that the spoken word travels through space, and continues to travel long after it was spoken. Jesus' 'yes' of Calvary was never intended to be a once-off word, but a word that would be repeated through time and eternity. 'You dare your "yes" and experience a meaning. You repeat your "yes" and all things acquire a meaning. When everything has a meaning, how can you live anything but a "yes"?' (Dag Hammerskold).

I cannot, and must not try to live today on a 'yes' of yesterday. Each day requires its own 'yes', and we are privileged indeed that we can connect into that word, and join our own 'yes' to the 'yes' of Jesus. Lucifer and, later, Adam and Eve had all said 'no', and Eucharist continues to be a resounding response to that. Calvary is a mountain from which flow the sacraments, like rivers of redemption, to wash us of our sins, and to satisfy our every thirst.

Calvary has merit only because of what resulted from it. The Eucharist begins when I come back out the door, having been commissioned to 'love and serve the Lord'. After Calvary, Mary gathered up the scattered flock of apostles, came down the hill, and waited for the result, or the resurrection. The Eucharist is a source of new life, because we receive the Bread of Life. Jesus speaks with great conviction, and at great length, about being the Bread of Life, and how essential it is for us to be nourished by that Bread. 'I am the bread of life; they who come to me shall never be hungry' (Jn 6:35). 'I am the bread which comes down from heaven ... It has been written in the Prophets: They shall all be taught by God' (Jn 6:41, 45).

Referring back to my concerns in a previous paragraph about the dearth of proper teaching on the Eucharist, I am becoming more convinced that, unless the Spirit of God is working powerfully through me, I could never hope to inspire anybody about anything of God, and that applies especially to a mystery such as Eucharist. 'Flesh and blood has not revealed this to you, but my Father who is in heaven' were Jesus' words to Peter, when Peter declared whom he knew Jesus to be. We are a Eucharistic people, and we are most united when we gather around the table of the Lord. Just as Calvary was a source for the sacraments, so Eucharist is a source of spiritual nourishment and nutrition. What a difference it would make to our church life if we gave proper and appropriate importance and emphasis to our celebration of Eucharist.

Calvary had every possible dimension of humanity. There was the human and the divine, the spotless Mary and the public thief. There was the Jew, the Roman and, no doubt, the Samaritan. There were tears and there was laughter and mockery. There was silence, and there was raucous noise. There seemed to be some kind of upheaval, as if hell was in revolt, and revolting graves threw up their dead. The veil protecting the Holy of Holies was torn in two, hardened soldiers quaked in fear, while the faithful mother and the beloved disciple looked on in silent anguish. How can I possibly celebrate Eucharist without my spirit being touched? 'Take off your shoes, because the ground on which you stand is holy.' Better not to begin if what follows is just a sleep-walk. We are all familiar with Jesus' saying about where two or more are gathered in his name, that he is there in the midst of them. If Jesus is present, then we can be sure that the Father and the Spirit are there as well. If the Trinity is present, then we need have no doubt that all of heaven is present.

Blessed Mother Teresa told a priest that I know: 'Celebrate this Mass as if it were your first Mass. Celebrate this Mass as if it were to be your last Mass. Celebrate this Mass as if it was the only Mass you were allowed celebrate in your whole life.' Yes, unfortunately, familiarity can breed indifference, and I can sleep-walk through the celebration like a robot that is programmed. I was given to understand, in my earlier life, that to miss Mass was a very serious sin. I am now just as concerned about the possibility to having to account for some of the Masses I attended.

Notice the word 'attended', rather than 'celebrated'. Not everybody on Calvary was concerned about Jesus, or had his best interests at heart. That is why I sometimes ask the people, at the beginning of Mass, to sit down for half a minute to reflect on why they're here. There's a story about a bishop, dreaming that he was preaching a sermon, and when he woke up, he discovered that he was!

I am a product of the Penny Catechism era. We memorised the answers, and we rattled off the definitions. If life has taught me anything it has taught me this: A time must come when I take personal responsibility for my life, for my beliefs, and for my actions. The shepherds of Bethlehem were told the news about Jesus by angels. However, they immediately said 'Let us go to Bethlehem, and see this thing for ourselves, which the Lord has made known to us.' That journey to the manger is symptomatic of the many many faith-journeys that each of us must make in our growth in Christian faith. The academic knowledge of the Penny Catechism has grown into the experiential knowledge of seeing for myself, and of finding out for myself.

The Spirit works away quietly, quite unknown to us most of the time. The process of gestation is mostly hidden, either in the womb, or with the seeds beneath the ground. And then, one day, the unborn moves, or the green shoots appear over the ground. If I were to try and detect the work of the Spirit in my own life, relative to appreciation of and love for the Eucharist, I would suggest that it happened during my time at the altar. I cannot think of any seminary course, or religious book that stirred my heart with a love for the Eucharist.

When I begin to take responsibility for my own life, and for my own faith, I will bring a more open, sincere, and attentive attitude to the altar when I celebrate Eucharist. I could no longer dismiss the Eucharist just because the celebrant failed to inspire or to entertain me. In a previous chapter, I longed for the day when the church would enthuse its members about preparing for Pentecost. Here again, I long for another day, when those with teaching or formation responsibility within the church will bring a zeal, an enthusiasm, and a genuine sense of urgency to the task of leading our people to a meaningful, Spirit-filled celebration of Eucharist. I can never hope in vain, when I believe that the Spirit has given me 'the hope that I have'.

What place does Mary have in our salvation?

It is my belief that to get a clear, honest, and accurate reply to this question, it is necessary to clear away much and many of the myths and 'devotions' of the past. It is necessary to rediscover Mary in such a way that, rather than have 'devotion' to her, I can develop a deep and personal *relationship* with her. She is not my Saviour, she is not my Redeemer. She did not, and does not, work miracles, but she certainly knows where to go to obtain miracles. She is not the centre of Christianity, but she certainly leads to the centre, points to Jesus who is the centre, and says to us, 'Do whatever he tells you.' Her unique place is to be the perfect role model for us in all that God calls or wants us to do.

I spoke in the last answer about the obedience of Jesus. Now I can speak about the obedience of Mary. The Archangel Gabriel came to her with a request from God. She questioned it in a natural, prudent, and common sense way. She would never respond unless she was sure that the message was from God. When the Archangel told her that the Holy Spirit would come upon her, and the power of the Most High would overshadow her, because there was nothing impossible with God, without hesitation, she answered her 'yes'. Later on, each of us would be asked the same question, and promised the same Spirit by God, and we really need Mary as a clear, uncomplicated model of exactly how we are asked to respond. It can be frightening to think that we can set limits to what God does for us in our lives, and God cannot work outside those limits. If, like Mary, I believe that 'nothing is impossible with God', then I will push back those limits, and remove them altogether.

When I speak about what God did in Mary, I am speaking of what God wishes to do through each one of us. If Adam and Eve's sin was one of pride, then Mary's greatest grace was that of humility. We speak of a proud person being 'full of herself/ himself'. Humility is something that is difficult to quantify. Any understanding I have of humility has been given me through some truly humble people I have met on the road of life. The example of their lives was so much more convincing, and so much easier to understand than anything I had read in a book, or heard in a homily. Carol Houselander speaks of Mary as being the 'reed of God'. When the reed is empty in the centre, and holes are made along the length of it, it is possible to make beautiful music by blowing one's breath down through the reed. Because Mary was open to the fullness of God's Spirit, that Spirit could play beautiful music through her, and produce something beautiful for God. Carol also compares Mary to a bird's nest, or a chalice that is empty, and is ready for whatever is chosen to place in it. The body of Jesus was placed within her, making her a monstrance, a tabernacle, an Ark of the Covenant. St Thérèse of Lisieux wrote about coming before God with empty hands. She had that approach during her lifetime, and that was how she expected to appear before God in death. It is more important to be in a receptive mood as I stand before God, rather than be conscious of all that I am giving.

In the answer to an earlier question, I spoke about the central importance of Pentecost in the life of the Christian. To appreciate Mary we have to think of her receiving her Pentecost at the very moment of conception. Jesus did not need to go down into the Jordan river to be baptised by John the Baptist, but he chose to. He wanted to identify with sinners from the very beginning. On the other hand, Mary was held up as a proto-type of what we could/would be like as a result of what Jesus and the Spirit would effect in and through us. I'm sure that, if I asked her why God chose her, and not someone else, she could answer that he chose her because he could have chosen anybody. She didn't/ couldn't take any personal pride from the fact that God chose her, because this was God's decision and his doing. Certainly, she deserves our thanks for co-operating with that decision. The poet called her 'our human nature's solitary boast'. Her humility came from the fact that she had a very sharp focused view of herself relative to God. No matter how perfect she might be, because of that very fact, she saw things as they were, because she was filled with the Spirit of Truth. She *magnified* the Lord, which simply means that her God was infinitely powerful, and there was nothing impossible for him. The bigger your God, the smaller your problems. It is not possible to separate her humility from her faith, because they are two sides of the same coin.

She had the unblemished view of the innocent, when she looked at reality. The contemplative is somebody who stares relentlessly at reality, and comes to discover what's really there. Because she saw things as they really were, she had no difficulty in knowing her place before God. Accepting my place before God is just another expression of humility. When it is patently obvious that, without God, I have nothing, or am nothing, it is much easier to have a humble heart. She trusted God unconditionally, and nothing could shake her belief that God would be totally faithful to all his promises. Elizabeth said to her 'All these things happened to you because you believed that the promises of the Lord would be fulfilled' (Lk 1:45). Jesus would later say 'The sin of this world is unbelief in me', and 'When the Son of Man comes will he find any faith on this earth?'

Mary asks two questions that are recorded in the gospels. She asked the Archangel Gabriel how she could become a mother, if she were still a virgin; and, when she found the boy Jesus in the Temple, she asked 'Why did you do this to us? Your father and I have been searching for you.' She may well have had many other questions, but once she began to realise that this was something that was away beyond human understanding, she asked no questions but, we're told, 'She kept all these things in her heart, and continually pondered over them' (Lk 2:19).

As Mary made her way to Egypt or to Calvary, I'm sure she had much to ponder in her heart. Calvary was probably her greatest test, but I am certain that she, and maybe she alone, had heard and believed the words of Jesus that he would rise from the dead, and come back to them. The apostles had heard those words also, of course, but obviously Jesus' promise was not enough for them.

In recent times, when it seemed as if the church had ended up back on Calvary, when the whole structures were falling apart, and when the glory days were over, I thank God that I heard Mary's assuring word that Easter was only around the corner. When that Calvary moment came, many of our people, like the apostles, took flight, and deserted what they saw as a sinking ship. Once again, she would have believed what we all have been told: 'There is nothing impossible for God.'

A few years ago I gave a six-day retreat to a community of Cistercian monks. Two of the monks had died suddenly on the same day, just a week prior to the retreat. I spoke of one of the great discoveries they may have made when they arrived in heaven. I told my listeners: 'They always knew this, but now they are certain of it: The scope and extent of what God did for them in their lives was determined by the limits they set, and God could not work outside of those limits.'

Mary has often had to stand by the cross of Jesus, as his Body, the church, went through yet another crisis that was considered as terminal. At Cana of Galilee she saw the crisis, went straight to Jesus with it, and then told the others to 'Do whatever he tells you.' It was blind faith, but it was deep faith. Many an artist has attempted to depict the desolation of this Mother on Calvary. No doubt it was a very dark moment, and her heart was breaking as she looked on. However, I like to think that her great love enabled her to be much more conscious of the sufferings Jesus had to endure, rather than anything she herself was experiencing. She certainly wasn't into self-pity in any way, because her concern for the welfare of others would predominate over any concern she might have for herself.

I find now that I can no longer speak of having a 'devotion' to Mary. Rather have I a personal relationship with her. I was truly blessed in the role model of mother that I had in my earthly mother. I was truly blessed through her, and now that both mothers are looking after me, I don't make any great distinction between either of them. I feel certain that both are with me now, and will be there 'at the hour of my death'. Both are very 'down-to-earth' in my life (one is my Mother, and the other is my mammy!). They stand on either side of me at the altar each day; they sit on chairs at either side of my bed at night. I would have claimed to know my biological mother very well, and I did. It fascinates me, however, to discover just how much she has grown in my mind and memory, and in my everyday life today. I have deliberately cultivated an awareness of the company of both mothers, and it matters not which of them helps me at any one time.

I go to Lourdes every year, and I love the grotto and the statue; but I can sit anywhere in the general environs and be very aware of her presence. To see all those people bring their sick to Our Mother is very moving, and I like to think that they all leave with a special blessing. I hold Medjugorje close to my heart as a place of great blessing, but the preoccupation of some people with signs and wonders, for example, is something that makes me very ill at ease. Mary herself said that the signs are for the unbelievers. Jesus said 'Unless you see signs and wonders, you will not believe.' On the other hand, of course, if I do believe, I very well can become quite used to signs and wonders.

I see an exact parallel between Mary at the Annunciation, and Mary at Pentecost. In both cases she was directly involved in providing the body of Christ. I don't think the apostles would have stayed for nine days in that Upper Room, waiting for the Spirit to come. Mary knew that her people had waited for many centuries for a Messiah to come. It is part of being poor to have to wait for hand-outs, or for whatever break might come along. They themselves can do very little to hurry up the process. I like to think that Mary was seen at her best in that Upper Room. When Jesus was preaching, she had to wait at the edge of the crowd, in the hope of having a word with him. Of course, the apostles were right there beside him, and were very conscious of their status as being part of his inner circle. After all that happened before and during Calvary, a very frightened group of men, very deflated and unsure of themselves, gathered with Mary in that Upper Room. Her compassion and kindness must have been palpable. There was no recrimination, no snide comments, no put downs. She spoke to them in such a way that their own faith was re-enkindled, and some kind of peace and hope began to seep into their hearts.

What Mary was doing now was just another form of gestation, as the body of Jesus was being formed, and all the parts being reconciled. Yes, indeed, that body had been badly broken in more ways than one, and Mary was confronted with the wounds. If you ever come across the body of Christ without the wounds, it's a phoney. Brokenness is part of what we are. (We're all cracked[!], and the Spirit enters through the cracks.) Jesus had returned to his Father, absolutely confident that his Mother would prepare the apostles for the completion of his mission.

As for you and me, it simplifies things if we place the two words Annunciation/Pentecost side by side, and see them as interchangeable. You can choose whichever word appeals to you, but the final outcome is the same: What happened to Mary must happen in us and who better to prepare our hearts for that than Mary herself? On the night before he died, Jesus gave us himself in Eucharist, and just minutes before he died on the cross, he gave us his Mother. St John, to whom Mary was entrusted, writes, 'And from that moment, the disciple took her to his own home' (Jn 19:27). Jesus' Mother is now mine, and I should make room for her in my home.

A word on the Rosary, which Mary has revealed as such a source of power and blessing. I remember a time in my life when I was puzzled that Mary seemed to be encouraging people to pray to her. This didn't match up with the humble little woman of the gospels. Naturally, of course, I readily accept that if Mary is in a place where she is given access to the treasuries of heaven, she is perfectly wise and loving to invite us to come to her … for our sakes. There is another dimension of the Rosary, however, that must be recognised. The Rosary is about Jesus. The Joyful Mysteries contain the promises of the gospels. The Sorrowful Mysteries display the price that Jesus paid, and that we must pay to enter into the kingdom. The Mysteries of Light highlight very special moments in the mission of Jesus. And the Glorious Mysteries proclaim the awards awaiting those who respond to the call of Jesus.

In generations past, when our people did not have Bibles, or may have been illiterate, the Rosary was the only Bible they had. For them, the Rosary was the gospel on their knees. The Annunciation is about a Saviour coming. Elizabeth is thrilled because Mary has brought Jesus to her; and the shepherds and Wise Men came to Bethlehem, not to meet Mary, but to find Jesus. The Rosary is a very special gift from Mary, because she uses it to get us so many and varied gifts from Jesus. The rosary beads is like a weapon, and our older generations never left the beads out of their hands, and the next-of-kin made sure that it was still in those hands as they were folded in the coffin.

The question was 'What place does Mary have in our Salvation?' I feel that I could never do justice to that question, but I trust, gentle reader, that what I have presented will convince you beyond all doubt that Jesus very definitely and deliberately includes his Mother as a very important part of the many blessings he bequeathed to us. 'I will not leave you orphans', he told us, and then he gave us his Father, and he gave us his Mother. He tells us then that it won't work unless we become like little children. Thank you, Jesus.

Is there such a thing as a 'Gift' of prayer?

I own nothing. Everything is gift. Life itself is a gift. One heart attack, and it's all over. Only God can do God things. Praying is a God-thing, and it is not the same as simply *saying prayers*. Saying prayers is usually using a prayer book and reading prayers that someone else wrote. This is as good a place as any to *start*, providing that I am willing to be led along the path of prayer, so that prayer becomes what the Spirit is doing in me. The organ God gave me with which to pray is my *heart*, and, if my heart is not praying, my tongue is wasting its time.

The apostles were with Jesus for three years. They came to know something of his thinking, of his habits, and of his likes and dislikes. They saw him raise the dead, calm the storm, cleanse the leper, and give sight to the blind. The one thing he did, however, that seemed to impress them most was when he prayed. That is why they came to him and said, 'Lord, teach us to pray.'

Jesus spent long hours and many long nights in prayer with the Father. It was after a night in prayer that he chose his apostles. His sermon on the Mount was preceded by a night of prayer and, in preparation for Calvary, he went to the Garden of Gethsemane to pray. Jesus said that he never said anything unless the Father told him to say it. It was during those times in prayer that the Father revealed his will to Jesus. When I go to bed at night-time, I have several gadgets, e.g. mobile phone, that I plug in to recharge during the night. That was how Jesus would have experienced prayer. Prayer means being in touch with the source, and Jesus is the one who puts me personally in touch with the Father. Prayer is, indeed, a gift, and it is one of God's most important and obvious gifts.

There is a family in the north of Ireland that I count among my special friends. There are two boys and a girl, ranging in age from fifteen to seventeen. They are very gifted in many ways, but particularly gifted at music. The eldest lad teaches the guitar, and the youngest and only girl teaches the piano. Besides the piano and a set of drums, you will find ordinary guitars, electric guitars, tin whistle, bódhrán, banjo, and bongo drums. I am certain that if I handed in a sitar or a xylophone to them today, they would be playing both instruments tomorrow. When I place myself alongside of that, and admit that I couldn't play a scale on any musical instrument, you will have a very clear image of what difference the gift of music makes. These young people have the gift of music to a very high degree, while I don't have any talent whatever in the field of music. I use this example to emphasise as strongly as I can just how difficult, if not impossible, it is to pray without having the gift of prayer. Once again, I distinguish between praying and saying prayers, just as I compare the full-blooded and free-flowing music these young people produce, and the feeble one-finger attempts I make at the piano. Trying to pray, without having the gift of prayer, can be a tedious and boring experience. St Paul tells us that we 'should pray without ceasing'. Such a thing would be completely impossible for anyone who does not have the gift of prayer.

Prayer is especially in the realm of the Spirit. I shouldn't attempt to pray without 'plugging in' to the Holy Spirit first. It is the Spirit in my words that turns them into prayer. Otherwise I am only saying words. I ask the Spirit of Truth to be in my heart that I may be sincere in what I say. St Paul tells us that the Spirit prays in us, and we can tune into that prayer, by going down into our hearts, becoming aware of the action of the Spirit, joining in it with goodwill, while not actually saying anything. After all, the keys of the piano do contribute something to the production of the music, and it's not all in the hands of the pianist. I offer the keys of willingness, giving the Spirit free and unlimited access to my mind, heart, and soul, and I allow myself to be led into prayer ... vocal, meditation, and contemplation. Prayer is a journey, and the Spirit leads us on that journey, as long as we are willing to be led. My 'yes' to the Spirit is at the heart of my prayer, and everything flows from that.

THE GIFT OF PRAYER

I should follow the example of the apostles and ask for the gift of prayer. I can never appreciate that gift until I receive it, and then, and only then, will I come to realise just how difficult, if not impossible, it had been to try to pray without the gift of prayer. The Lord can read our hearts like an open book. If I ask for the gift of prayer, it will be very obvious to the Lord whether I really want that gift or not. Mary tells us that 'he fills the hungry with good things'. Ralph Martin, one of the earlier leaders in the spread of Charismatic Renewal, wrote a masterpiece at the time, entitled *Prayer is a Hunger*. It is, indeed, and it certainly satisfies the hungry heart.

There is nothing automatic about having a gift. Having the gift of being a painter will never make me paint a picture. My young friends, to whom I referred earlier, may be greatly gifted with the gift of music, but they certainly make use of this in many long hours of lessons, practice, and experiment. They have the gift, but they are responsible for developing that gift. They have the gift to begin with, of course, and then they proceed to use that gift, just as they did with their gift of speech, walking, reading, or writing. It may be easy, because they have the gift, but it can still involve long hours of hard work. I learned to walk by walking, and to talk by talking. I learn to pray by praying. Watching an Olympic gold medallist touch the tape in the 100 metres dash can take one's breath away. It is easy to forget that this person had to begin with that first faltering step. There has been a huge investment of time and energy between that first faltering step, and touching the tape in the 100 metres dash. All of this has happened, it seems, because this person discovered that he had the gift to run with such speed, and it was up to him to develop that gift.

We are truly doubly-gifted when we discover the centrality of prayer, and that we can receive a gift to make it possible for us to pray. Prayer is like a path of discovery, and it will always lead me into something new. Like the young person with the gift for music, I will soon find myself venturing into writing my own songs. I won't need the prayerbook any more. I have watched one of these lads spend hours just plucking at the guitar, trying combinations of sounds ... and all in the search for a new melody. Most professional singers today (as against the classical opera stars) write their own songs. When someone does that, it is hoped that the melody range is within the singer's competence, and the words convey what the singer needs to say. The gift of prayer, of course, is not always about striking out in search of something new. I can have a lilt in my voice, and a song in my heart as I recite the psalms in the Prayers of the Church (Office). It is this gift of prayer that prevents the Rosary becoming a boring repetition of words. Without this gift, such repetition can be boring, and very uninspiring.

I myself find that this gift of prayer is most helpful when I stand at the altar for Mass. Repeating the same prayers day after day, for the duration of one's lifetime, can easily become lifeless and shallow. It is only by using the gift of prayer that I have in my heart that I can hope to have any kind of enthusiasm within me. I always begin Mass by inviting the Spirit to be in my words and actions, and I ask Mary, caretaker of my heart, to come with me to the altar, and help me join my 'yes' to Jesus' to his 'yes' to the Father.

The more I write about this gift of prayer, the more convinced I am that it is foolhardy and irresponsible to try to pray without it. I know people who cannot speak; I know people who cannot see. I know people who cannot walk, and I know people who cannot read. It is obvious to me that, barring a miracle, there is nothing that can be done to alter their condition. If I told a blind man that I had found a secret that enabled him to see, do you think he would be interested in what I had to offer? I speak directly to you, gentle reader, as I speak about the gift of prayer.

The Holy Spirit came to complete the mission of Jesus. It is as if Jesus took on the enemy in an external way, while the Spirit works quietly away from within. In the letter to the Romans we are told that our salvation depends on 'his blood, and our faith'. In other words, it depends on what Jesus has done, and what we are prepared to do about that. Our response to what Jesus has done includes our prayer life. It is the Spirit who makes it possible for us to respond. The initiative is taken by the Father, when he sends Jesus to us. This is followed through by Jesus, as he carries out his mission. Then the Spirit comes to dwell in us, so that, with the help of the Spirit, we can respond to the offer of salvation, and come to the fullness of grace. In other words, our role in the whole proceedings is quite minor, but essential. God does his part, and sends the Spirit to enable us do our part. Only God can do a God-thing, and prayer is one of those very special 'God-things'. No wonder the apostles asked Jesus to teach them to pray.

The Gifts of the Spirit include Wisdom, Discernment, Knowledge, and Faith, among others. Prayer is certainly one of those Gifts, and it is something that should be eagerly sought for by all of God's people, so we can avail of the many blessings and graces that are made available through prayer. Unfortunately, I have not heard any great stress being laid on the necessity of this gift in our lives. It is as if we just 'plough ahead' (in quiet desperation!), saying prayers, whether we're 'prayerful' or not. This is a great pity, because I never cease to be amazed by the goodwill and effort put into prayer by people of goodwill. Without being helped to discover and obtain the gift of prayer, I think of them pushing a car along a road, up hills, and down dales ... simply because nobody bothered to tell them about the engine, and the ignition key!

It is reasonable to assume that the Spirit is more than willing and ready to give this gift to those who ask. Paul tells us that we don't know how to pray, but that the Spirit prays in us, just as Jesus says that the Spirit will give us the words whenever we speak on his behalf. I cannot overstress the basic truth that this is *all* the work of God, from beginning to end. Sometimes the Lord is working directly, and sometimes he is working through us.

I was in a house recently where one of the girls was going away to do a course in another part of the country. The course would take a few months. The parents bought her a mobile phone, which they set up for her, and arranged with the local bank for a standing order payment. Her parents needed to hear from her regularly, so they provided the means for her to do that. The Holy Spirit is so much more than a mobile phone! I use this analogy simply to point to the fact that Jesus ensured that we could still make contact with base, in heaven, after he returned there. The Holy Spirit would be our umbilical chord, and our spirits would draw all their sustenance from heaven.

Yes, indeed, 'not on bread alone do we live'. We are human beings who have been elevated to living with the spirit of the Divinity. 'So then, if you are risen with Christ, seek the things that are above, where Christ is seated at the right hand of God. Set your minds on things above, not on earthly things. For you have died, and your life is now hidden with Christ in God' (Col 3:1-3).

Working with human resources keeps us functioning on the human level. This is just as life would be if Jesus had never come among us. However, life is different now. The coming of Jesus, and his sending the Spirit has changed things utterly. This is most evident in prayer. 'We do not speak of wisdom to the mature in faith, although it is not a wisdom of this world, or of its rulers, who, by the way, come to nothing. We teach the mystery and secret plan of divine wisdom … God has revealed it to us, through his Spirit, because the Spirit probes everything, even the depth of God … No one but the Spirit knows the secrets of God … He who remains on the human level does not understand the things of the Spirit' (1 Cor 2:6-7, 10, 14).

My answer, in summary, is this: It would be wrong, as well as impossible, for us to continue our life of prayer without asking for the gift to do so. It would be wrong and impudent for us to continue attempting to do something that is totally the preserve and action of the Spirit. Lord, teach us to pray … Spirit of God, please gift us the gift of prayer … Mary our Mother, caretaker of our hearts, please pray in us, for us, with us, and obtain for us the gift of prayer.

How can I live in the 'Now'?

It is quite usual to hear people bemoaning the ills of the world today, and the apparent problematic condition of the church. They speak of the 'good old days', and long for their return. They fail to take on board one vital ingredient in this evaluation of things: The Plan of God. God, in his infinite wisdom, decided that one hundred years ago was not a good time for me to be on this planet earth, or to be a member of his church. He also decided, in his infinite wisdom, that one hundred years from now would not be a good time for me to be on this planet, or in his church. In his infinite wisdom he decided that now was the best possible time for me to be around! This should cause me to look around again at the world in which I live, and the church to which I belong, take a deep breath, and say 'Yes', and bloom where I'm planted!

It is important that I live in reality, and not in some world of make-believe, of has-been, or of might-be. The only time that exists is *now* and, if I'm ever going to do anything with my life, I should do it now. 'I shall pass this way but once. Any good deed that I can do, any good word that I can say, let me do it now, let me say it now, because I'll never pass this way again.' Life is not manageable. One heart attack, and it's all over. When I worry about life, I have no idea whether I'm worried about thirty years or ninety years! Life is made up of packages of 24-hours, and the secret of living is to keep things within the day. Today has enough worries of its own!

The first thing I have to do, if I wish to live in the 'now', is to get out of the past. Time that has passed is gone, and will never return. It is a time that no longer exists. 'Lord, give me the serenity to accept the things I cannot change.' There are *two* things that I cannot change: I cannot change yesterday, nor can I change another human being. *The only value the past has are the lessons it taught me.* I would be a very wise person, indeed, if I learned every lesson that life has taught me. History is, quite often, a repeat of people repeating the mistakes of a previous generation. (Some years ago it was Vietnam, now it is Iraq!) If I cannot change the past, that implies that I have no control over it. What, then, can I do with it? When Jesus died on Calvary, his death extended back to Adam and Eve, and made it possible to reclaim and redeem all that was placed in bondage since then. Jesus can transform the past. He can turn evil into good. 'Oh happy fault, that merited so great a Redeemer!' was the exclamation of St Augustine.

All of the failures of my past can be turned into compassion, empathy, and tolerance. Compassion is not something one can learn from a book. It is learned from our own brokenness, failures, and sins. There is an Arab definition of a friend that applies very well to Jesus: 'A friend is someone to whom one can pour out all the contents of one's heart, wheat and chaff together, knowing that gentle hands will sift it, keep what is worth keeping and, with the breath of love, will blow the chaff away.' The good Lord garners the nuggets of wisdom that life has taught, entrusts those to me, asking me never to lose them and, with the breath of love, he blows the rest away. Anyone of us can admit to the following: There are things 'back there' that we wished had not happened. There are events that embarrass us to recall. There are things of which we are ashamed, and that cause some nagging guilt. When this process is handled properly, and Jesus is really accepted as *Saviour* in my life, all of that guilt, regret, remorse, shame, and embarrassment is gone. We accept the lessons we have learned, and we move on with grateful hearts, and with renewed hope. An important part of God's forgiveness of our sins is the removal of all negative memories connected with them. In other words, he heals all of me. Forgiving my sins, and letting me go down the road, filled with guilt and shame, would not be complete forgiveness. The Lord doesn't do half-jobs! He completes what he begins. Jesus asks the question 'Who do you say that I am?' I will not find the answer in a book; it is to be found only within the human heart. If he is Saviour, it means that I have entrusted *all* of my past to him, and he takes care of it. That care includes forgiving and healing. Because my past is in his hands, I will never have to account for it. If it is in his hands, it is redeemed, and he has conferred on me the gift of salvation, the grace to start again. Salvation is a truly wonderful gift. It is not something I'll get when I die. Rather it is the grace given me by God to start again any moment I choose. I can start again at any moment of my life. 'Today is the beginning of the rest of your life.'

'Who do you say that I am?' The second part of the answer to this question has to do with the future. If I entrust my future to his care, then he is Lord. Just as the past no longer exists, so the future does not exist yet. It is not mine, I cannot presume it, or try to control it. Most of the worries that I see in the future will probably never actually happen, and there is no guarantee that I will be alive to experience them, if they do happen. I can never be sure what is coming next; it could be tomorrow, or it could be eternity. I don't know which will come first. If I accept Jesus as Lord of my life, I can hand the future into his care. I need have no worry what the future holds, if he holds the future.

I received a gift this morning, the gift of today. It has never before been given to anyone, and it will never again be given to anyone. Because it is a gift, is that why we call it the present?! Written on the gift are the words 'batteries included'. There is nothing going to happen today that the Lord and myself will not be able to handle. St Teresa of Avila says, 'Teresa, on her own, can do nothing. Teresa and two ducks can do nothing. Teresa, two ducks, and God, can do anything.'

With each day is given the 'daily bread' to live that day. Accepting the gift of life in separate 24-hour 'packages', helps to make it liveable. 'Keep life within the day' is good advice, indeed. Jesus wants me to walk with him. He doesn't want me to linger in the past, with guilt and regret, or to run ahead into the future, with worry and anxiety. The only real time is now. A young woman told me recently that she had just joined the St Vincent de Paul Society in her parish, but she was unsure if this was the right time to do so, as her children are quite young. I smiled, as I told her that the best time to do anything like that is now, because most people are going to do something 'next Monday'! There is nothing more powerful than an idea whose time has come. There is no scarcity of ideas, and we are told that 'The road to hell is paved with good intentions.' And again, 'Procrastination is the thief of time.' I become proactive when I become a person of now, and things begin to get done.

Bad habits die slowly. It may take more than a while to correct the habit of anticipating worries, always waiting for the other shoe to drop. However, there is wonderful freedom to be obtained by living in the now, and taking time out to smell the flowers. 'Life is a mystery to be lived, not a problem to be solved' (Thoraeu). Life doesn't respond very well to the 'white-knuckle' approach, which is certainly not compatible with living and walking in the Spirit. God is in control, and he doesn't lie awake at night worrying about us! Neither does he want us to be awake at night worrying about ourselves.

There is a third part of the answer to the question, 'Who do you say that I am?' Jesus is Saviour in my life that is past, and he is Lord of my life yet to come. The third part is that he is God in the now. God is totally a God of now. 'I am who am.' God has no past, or no future. He lives in the eternal *now*, where all time is present to him as if it were a moment. 'A thousand years in your sight is just like yesterday.' 'There is nothing impossible for God'. That is my God of now. If I could become a person of now, I would meet God.

Unfortunately, many people meet God for the first time when they die. It is then that the running, the hiding, the blaming, the denying is all over, and they stand before God exactly as they are. 'Now is the acceptable time; today is the day of salvation.' I could and should pray for the grace to live in the now. I should pray for the grace to be free of the guilt of the past, and the worries of the future. I should try to develop a sense of 'contentedness' in the presence of God now, because that will form the basis of my relationship with him for all eternity. God is fully

present to me right here, right now, and I should try to recipro-
cate that presence. It makes no sense not to be in the present
when I pray.

Supposing I am giving a talk to a group of people in a room.
There are three things that I should remember: The most important people in the world for me now are gathered in this room,
because I am not speaking to anybody else; the most important
place for me in the whole world, is this room, because I am not
anywhere else; and the most important time in my whole life is
now, because it is the only time that exists for me at this moment.
The combination of these three points ensures that I am totally
present to others.

It is said about people from time to time, 'He is very scattered
… she is all over the place … and he needs to get himself together.' The opposite to that is 'togetherness', 'wholeness', or what is
sometimes called 'holiness'. Striving to become an authentic
person is a very laudable ambition, and the kind of presence I
bring to others or to my work is a clear indicator of how authentic a person I am. It is only when I am being authentic that I am a
life-giving person. Being authentic in my presence, my listening,
and my 'centredness' is at the core of caring.

The question under consideration in this chapter is 'How can
I live in the Now?' It is much easier to answer this question than
to actually do what is required. Bad habits tend to linger, and because they were built up over a number of years, they are not
going to be changed overnight. I consider it one of the gifts of
the Spirit to 'anchor' me in the now, because it betokens a level
of contented peace that is 'not like the peace that the world
gives', as Jesus said. Being anchored in the now is a reflection of
one of the divine attributes, just as God is totally present to me at
every moment of every day.

There are so many blessings resulting from the use of this gift
that it should be sought with great eagerness and sincerity by all
of God's people. In exercising this gift I become an attentive lis-
tener, a sincere and genuine speaker, and a real and warm
friend. The acquiring and practice of this gift can transform a

personality for the better, and all those around can benefit from it. Yes, indeed, nothing but good can come from becoming a person of the 'now', and when it comes to our relationship with God, it is more than just something to be desired. It is something that is part of any worthwhile relationship, either with God or with others. I have seldom heard it spoken about in a homily, or written about in a book, and I genuinely think that that is a great pity. I hope what I have written makes some amends for this.

I am writing purely from the Christian/religious perspective, but everything I have written could help everybody, of all religions and none. Living my life within the constant tension between the past and the future must cause great wear and tear to the nervous system. I am on a cross of my own making, with one arm stretched out to change the past, and the other stretched out to arrange the future. There is so much nervous energy going into this, that there is very little of me left in the present! It must be difficult, if not impossible, to develop worthwhile relationships, or creative talent, while there is so little of me present in the process. To practise and to achieve living in the 'now', could bring me to a life beyond my wildest dreams.

What's special about the adoration of the Blessed Sacrament?

A simple and direct answer to that question is: Jesus is truly present there, he wants us to be with him, and we are blessed abundantly with that privilege. It is for our sakes, and for our sakes only, that Jesus makes himself present in the Eucharist.

Unfortunately, my early experience of this was not good, and I've had quite a difficulty in coming to appreciate, and avail of the blessings of the Presence. My earlier memories of Benediction or 'Forty Hours' was one of hard work. There were flowers, candles, thuribles, incense, and endless songs, and long, long prayers! I remembered it as something to be endured, rather than enjoyed, and I'm sure that the person of Jesus was smothered amidst all the pomp and religious ceremony. It is only in relatively recent times that I have woken up to the extraordinary blessing that it is to be able to spend real time in the company of Jesus, without any obligation to *do* anything but just *be*.

Even if, like the apostles in Gethsemane, I doze off, all is well, and nothing but good ensues. If I have been busy, and feeling tired, there is nothing Jesus would like more than that I should 'come aside and rest awhile'. Despite the difficulties I had with this devotion in my early life, I have always had a warm spot in my heart for what we called 'visits' to the Blessed Sacrament. These were short, didn't require much praying (!), and were usually prompted by an urgent cry for help for an upcoming exam!

The background to all this is God's ability to be present to us in any way he chooses. To Moses, he could be in the burning bush. For the Israelites he was in the cloud by day, and the fire by night. To the Jews he was in the Holy of Holies, and to other religions he could be worshipped in the sun, or through many facets of nature. What matters is the *presence*. It is not just God's ability to be present, but his great willingness to be with us, and among us. God, of course, who is everywhere, is always with us, but it greatly helps that one of his ways of being present to us can be clearly identified and appropriately acknowledged.

I am not an historian, so I can only conjecture how this devotion evolved and developed over the years. In the early days of the church, the host (or 'bread') contained the Living Presence of the Lord for the duration of the Mass, but was not revered as an object of devotion outside of that time. During the early persecutions of the church, hosts were retained after Mass, to be brought to those in prison. While awaiting the time of distribution, they were stored in some sort of safe, which we now know as a tabernacle. Very early on, people gathered before this tabernacle to pray, and thus the Eucharistic devotion, as we know it, evolved. Obviously, this was confirmed by the Lord through many blessings received and, over time, this became a canonised form of devotion, given great importance in the order of things.

Very early on, it took on the form of reparation, where the general malaise and neglect of God could, somehow, be compensated for by people of goodwill and good heart. This reparation dimension is very much part of this devotion today, and it's what motivates many of the devotees who make a particular vocation out of adoration of the Blessed Sacrament. This is very commendable, and must be a source of many and great blessings to those involved and, through them, to the rest of us.

'Could you not watch one hour with me?' is a very sad question. Jesus values our presence and, while one of his disciples was making plans to betray him, he wanted the others to stay with him and be a source of consolation to him. It could be argued that Jesus doesn't need our company. On the other hand, however, if we understand what loves means, then we must accept that love always yearns to be met by love. Unrequited love is a most painful human experience.

Right from the beginning of this answer, I wish to stress that the church considers this devotion as being central and essential for the spiritual life of its people. Recent times have seen a revival of this devotion. With the almost disappearance of

Benediction and Forty Hours from our parish calendar, it was thought that devotion to the Blessed Sacrament was consigned to the past, like many other devotions of my youth. It now is obvious that this is not what the Spirit of God wants for the church.

In a most extraordinary way, this devotion underwent a revival in many different parts of the world at the same time. In my own country, Ireland, Perpetual Adoration began in several of our churches in different parts of the country, without any consultation with each other. The people felt a need for prayer; for something that would put them directly in touch with Jesus, without the need for theological education, or expertise in prayer techniques. There are many parishes in Ireland where ordinary country people are seen to enter the local church in the wee hours of the morning to 'do their hour' before the Blessed Sacrament. This has become part of their lives, and an accepted part of the local parish life. This must surely be the Spirit at work. These people have volunteered to be available, so that this devotion is continued and maintained among them.

All corporal works of mercy must be backed up by spiritual works of mercy. The Active and the Contemplative complement each other. Contemplative Prayer is the highest form of prayer, and sitting in the Presence of Jesus in the Eucharist is the perfect setting for such prayer.

An earlier question about prayer being a gift is very central to what we're talking about now. Of course, there are many good and useful books available to help one during this time of prayer. However, they run the risk of being seen as 'fillers' to help while away the hour. That, of course, is quite acceptable as a start, but it would not be advisable to continue with this kind of prayer. To be present with Jesus, to be in the presence of Jesus, is to be present at a School of Prayer. 'Lord, teach us to pray.' This is an ideal time for such a prayer, and an ideal time for such a prayer to be answered. With each visit, I may begin to notice myself on a journey, where the structure of my prayer begins to change and evolve. There is no way that we can predict where this may lead us, nor should we try to control or direct it in any particular way. Our main role is to show up, and leave the rest to the Lord, the God of Surprises.

Obviously, the first thing I must do, of course, is to come before the Lord exactly as I am. It may take some time to bring my own real presence before the Real Presence. I should get in touch with how I feel, and be consciously aware of every feeling, emotion, and thought within me. This is what the Lord sees when he looks at me, so there's no point in pretending, denying, excusing, or blaming. Prayer becomes so much easier when I am totally honest. I do not have to 'make up' anything. Just imagine you walk into the presence of Jesus with a prayer mat under your arm. The first thing you do is open the prayer mat out fully. You should do the same with your inner self. Out, out, out to the very edges, exactly as you are, with the good, the bad, the ugly. You have nothing more to give the Lord but that, plus, of course, the goodwill that brought you here in the first place. And, of course, you must realise that that is exactly all the Lord wants from you. Before you open your mouth, he thanks you for coming.

'Stay here, and keep watch with me'. 'Watch and pray that you enter not into temptation.' 'Could you not watch one hour with me?' I believe it is these words of Jesus that have inspired this particular form of devotion. I am both humbled and edified when I see those decent, hard-working country folk arriving on a bicycle at their local church in the wee hours of the morning. Unfortunately, life in our cities today makes such a situation impossible, as the church remains locked throughout the day, and is open for Mass, but not to the general public, who might want to call by for a prayer during the day. There is no point in moaning over this; we just have to get around it, and do the best we can. The danger of becoming too negative is that we end up doing nothing.

There are so many dimensions, and so many possibilities to this form of spirituality that I hesitate to mention some, and give the impression that I exclude the others. 'Whatever rows your boat.' There is no one way better than another, if I am present to the Lord and prayerfully aware of his presence. For a period of time, say for a few weeks, I may choose a particular path of prayer. For a week or two it may be adoration, and nothing else. I bow my soul before the Lord, or I prostrate myself in spirit, and say nothing. I am conscious of being surrounded by the angels as I do this, and I rejoice in their songs of adoration. This prayer of adoration can be combined with the prayer of thanksgiving, which also gives glory to the Lord.

On other occasions it can be petition, *lectio divina* (slow pondering on scripture passages), or simply listening. This can become a very exciting time, because the possibilities are endless when one sits with the Lord. If I have the charism of service, I could come before the Lord on behalf of all suffering people, or on behalf of the world. This is Christianity at its best, because it is entirely unselfish, as I am praying for people who will never know to thank me. More than anything else I must consciously and continually ensure that the initiative is with the Lord. 'Speak, Lord, your servant is listening' should always take precedence over 'Listen, Lord, your servant is speaking.'

For those who say a lot of prayers, it may take time before I begin to hear the Lord speak to me. However, if I continue to listen, I can be sure that his voice will come through. I'm not speaking of an audible voice here, of course, but I get a thought, an insight, or a sense of presence that is as real as if a voice had spoken to me. This is something that should be eagerly sought for, providing we are patient, and prepared to wait for the Lord to speak. It may sound like a contradiction, but the Lord is waiting on us to be ready to listen! There can be a lot of settling down needed within the human spirit before one can hear the gentle whispers of the Spirit. Prayer is not so much a question of me talking to God who doesn't hear, but God talking to me who won't listen!

I know an elderly lady who is bed-ridden, and she spends most of her waking hours in the presence of Jesus in the Blessed Sacrament. The church is a few miles away, but she bridges that gap in her imagination, and she makes herself present to the Lord. What a beautiful heart she must have! Speaking of imagination, this is something I can really use in this kind of prayer. I

can sit before the tabernacle, close my eyes, and let my imagination guide me in this encounter with the Lord. If Jesus is in
front of me, then I can close my eyes, and try to imagine what he
looks like. I can imagine him coming to sit beside me. What do I
want to say to him? What is he saying to me? Do you want to go
for a walk with him in the grounds of the church? Is there someone you know who is in hospital? Bring Jesus to that person, and
watch as he places a hand on that person's head. There is no
limit to the possibilities of this personal encounter. Use of the
creative imagination can be very powerful in prayer such as
Adoration. Both Jesus and yourself are fully alive, so the encounter can be a very lively one.

Another image that can help is to think of the incoming tide.
Jesus is the tide, and I am the beach. The beach puts no obstacle
in the way of the incoming tide. The beach will be totally transformed in the process. All the rubbish on the beach will be col-
lected and brought back out to sea. All the sea-life will arrive,
and all the worms in the sand will surface. The beach will come
to life, by doing nothing, apart from allowing the tide to come in,
and to go back out again. I can just be, and whisper my 'yes' to
the action of Jesus. Like the beach, I too will be changed each
time I allow this to happen.

For those who don't understand, no words are possible, and
for those who do understand, no words are necessary. That is
surely true about devotion to the Blessed Sacrament. It is very
much a 'come and see' situation. When the apostles asked Jesus
where he lived, he simply replied 'Come and see.' We are told
that they went with him, and spent the whole day with him.

There is a process of growth involved in this devotion.
Prayer could be defined as 'working on my relationship with
God'. This devotion certainly has a lot of the qualities of a grow-
ing relationship within it. I cannot recommend it too highly, and
I am totally confident that, for the person who is willing to begin
this form of prayer, it will lead directly to the eternal Presence of
Jesus in heaven. It is an extraordinary gift, and truly blessed are
they who discover this 'pearl of great price'.

How can I best use the Bible?

At the very beginning of my answer, there is one thing I need to stress. The Bible is the Word of God, and only God can explain his word. It is inspired writing. What I mean by that is that the Holy Spirit is in every word, and when I read the Bible, the Holy Spirit can enter my heart through the words that I read.

Let me put it another way. If I am reading obscene and pornographic material, or material that is intended to generate hatred, racism, and violence, how do you think that reading will affect me? The spirit that inspired the words, be that the Holy Spirit or an evil spirit, will enter my heart through the words that I read. Under normal circumstances, the person who picks up a Bible for the first time is someone, however young, who has been taught from this book over a period of time and is now ready to read it for herself. It would help to have an overview of the Bible before sitting down to read.

It contains the story of God's dealings with his people. The Old Testament (before the time of Jesus) could be compared to radio; while, from the coming of Jesus onwards (New Testament), could be compared to television. Continuing that image, it could be said that the living church is three-dimensional.

For the newcomer to the Bible, I would strongly advise beginning with the gospels. Without having any training in hermeneutics or exegesis (big words that refer to bible study!), it is easy to read about an incident in the gospel, to reflect on it, and learn about Jesus as he interacts with the sick, the sinner, or the religious leader. I can gain a lot from this kind of reading, without the help of others. However, if I seriously intend taking up Bible study, then I should join a Christian group who do this on a regular basis. Chances are they have qualified teachers on a regular basis, and they point to resource books that supply commentaries on Bible passages.

The Bible has been a bone of contention between Roman

Catholics and Protestants for a long time now. The Bible is an essential part of the Protestant 'prayer books', i.e. the book you carry under your arm on your way to church. It is only recently that the Bible has begun to appear in the hands of Roman Catholics. Catholics were discouraged from reading the Bible, for fear of wrong interpretation. The Protestant was encouraged to read the Bible regularly, and to have freedom in its interpretation. When you pick up a Catholic and a Protestant Bible, the Catholic one is the one with copious footnotes, and columns of commentaries down the side of the page. This is to ensure a proper (Catholic!) interpretation of the passage.

Whether Protestant or Catholic, I strongly recommend that your interest in the Bible should be dealt with maturely and responsibly. It can be a source of much blessings, and can have a real power for good, and a wonderful influence on my life. I recommend that you find a Bible study group of good standing, that is, preferably attached to your own church, or of your own denomination.

From the very beginning make a direct connection between Bible Study and your prayer life. We don't study the Bible looking for knowledge, as you would a history book, or an almanac. Our reading of the Bible is a very real expression of our openness to God. It is the work of the Spirit to reveal the Bible to me. 'Reveal' comes from the French, and it literally means to 'lift off the veil'. It is more a question of God revealing than me learning.

Some time ago a former KGB agent was poisoned in London by a deadly poison known as Polonium 10. This poison is so lethal that there are traces of it to be found wherever this agent had been during the days before his death. His home is still quarantined, and it may never be habitable again. This is a rather over-kill example to use, when trying to explain the opposite effect. The Word of the Lord is shot through and through with his Spirit, and that Word brings blessings wherever it goes.

When I go to Mass, I discover that it consists of the Liturgy of the Word, and the Liturgy of Eucharist. Both are equally important. In my younger days, I could be late for the Liturgy of the

Word, arrive in time for the Offertory, and I was deemed to be 'on time' for Mass! This could not be accepted today. Yves Congar OP, an influential contributor to Vatican II, says that if one parish had the Liturgy of the Word only, and another parish had the Liturgy of the Eucharist only, the one with the Liturgy of the Word is the one that becomes a Christian community. This is something that needs to be stressed, so that readers, homilists, and listeners might be more aware of their great responsibility. It is easy to forget that the nearest many of our people come to Bible Study is listening to the readings at Mass, or to the commentary that may be the centre of the homily that follows those readings. Is it unrealistic to think that such readings and homily might cause someone to run home, get out a Bible, and read those passages for themselves, with whatever commentaries may accompany them? There should be a conscious effort to bridge the gap between what happens in church, and what might happen in the home. It is a sad commentary if they remained totally unconnected. If the Bible is given the place it deserves, every opportunity should be availed of to inspire people to see the Bible as the source of living water that it is. The celebrant of the Eucharist should be a channel, rather than a generator or transformer, controlling the supply. Like John the Baptist, he should continually be pointing to Jesus, telling people where he may be found. The Bible is one such place.

To become 'familiar' with the Bible, to see it as a source for my prayer life and my spiritual formation, is a very precious and worthwhile gift to acquire. Some people are illiterate, and reading the Bible is beyond their ability. For those who can read, however, I strongly recommend that they take seriously all the riches and blessings that are available to us in the Bible. All of us, indeed, should check the place the Bible plays in our Christian formation. It should be placed alongside the salt and pepper condiments on the kitchen table. There should be a copy of the Bible or, at least, the gospels, on the locker by each bed. There are some excellent children's editions of the Bible, beautifully illustrated, and made attractive to the reader. The daily missal, and the Sunday missal provide an opportunity for us to prepare ourselves before we go to church. This will serve to create a connection between the home and what happens in church. On a Sunday, I can bring the Mass leaflet home with me for further reflection and, indeed, I could file it for future reading, as part of my prayer life.

There are no limits to the number and variety of booklets available today, with reflections and commentaries on the gospels. I am very aware of this great area of riches because, over the years, I myself have contributed several such books to the collection. Many of these booklets are deliberately published as pocket-size, to facilitate the possibility of it being on one's person at any free moment that comes along.

Several years ago, the 'Little Red Book' of Chairman Mao was the 'in' thing for the radical and the rebellious. Reading it at bus stops, in cafeterias, etc. was a status symbol! Both Mao and his book have long gone, but I use this as an example of what use I wish might be made of the Bible. In today's world, as we witness the spread of Islam, we can see how they give constant publicity to the Koran, and how reading the Koran is seen as central to their religious beliefs. In my younger days, the Bible was a very big, heavy book, given as a wedding present, in which some family details were recorded, and it was then placed on a shelf to gather dust for at least another generation. Its value came from it becoming part of the family inheritance! I thank my God that I have lived to see the end of that era. Slowly but surely, the Bible is being placed back in the hands of Catholics, and there is a growing awareness of how precious and blessed a gift it is.

I can read the Old Testament as the history of the Jewish people or, more correctly, I can read it as evidence of how God worked with, for and among his people. I can make a direct connection between the Old and the New Testaments, as I become aware of coming events throwing their shadows. Moses leading the people out of slavery, and into the Promised Land is a foreshadowing of the mission of Jesus. The Jewish Passover meal foreshadowed the Eucharist, and the Ten Commandments, (all negative, telling what *not* to do), were replaced by the two positive commandments about love of God and love of neighbour.

In answer to an earlier question, I wrote about what the gospels tell us about God, so I won't go into that here. I do want to stress, however, what the gospel incidents can mean for us today. There are two things that I must always keep in mind: *The gospels are today, and I am every person in the gospels.* When I begin to apply those two points, it changes everything. At one stage of my life I am the Prodigal Son; at another, his self-righteous brother; and I am called to become the Forgiving Father. I am every one of the apostles, including Judas, at different stages of my life. I have my own blindness, deafness, leprosy, and demons. There was a very helpful commentary on gospel incidents some years ago, called *That Man was You* (Juan Arias). It placed each of us, men and women, in different scenes of the gospels, and involved us directly in what happened. It helped to make the incident relevant, and the message more personal.

To understand Jesus' teaching, it is necessary to hear it with the mind of his listeners. They knew all about sheep, boats, fig trees, fishing nets, etc. They understood him when he spoke. He spoke with authority, and I can pay particular attention to that authority in his voice.

I had the great privilege of bringing groups on pilgrimage to the Holy Land on nine occasions. These were wonderful times for all of us. As we walked in the footsteps of Jesus, the gospel incidents became alive for us. For a few shekels extra, the boatman would stop the boat on the Sea of Galilee for an hour or two, while we read about the storms, the catch of fish, Jesus walking on the water, or Peter's aborted attempt to copy him. Our married couples renewed their vows in Cana, and left the bus and walked in twos for the last mile into Emmaus. I always enjoyed Bethany, where Jesus used to spend the odd weekend relaxing with his friends Martha, Mary, and Lazarus. Reading the gospels was never the same after spending twelve days wandering through these sacred places. Members of the groups often told me of the difference it made on a Sunday, as they sat in their local church, listening to the gospel being read during Mass. 'I was there' was their silent whisper!

Some years ago I gave a present of a Bible to a lady who really wanted to become familiar with it, but who felt totally inadequate, and was convinced that she would not be able to understand it. I gave her a copy of *The Living Bible*, which is written in plain everyday English. I advised her to read St John's Letters first.

The gospel of John is a very theological dissertation, with images of life/death, darkness/light, good/evil, etc. It begins like a volcanic eruption: 'In the beginning was the Word, and the Word was with God, and the Word was God ...' It is a gospel that was written in response to those who tried to deny the divinity of Jesus. There are more commentaries written on John's gospel than all other three put together.

It is remarkable, therefore, to follow the journey of John's life, until he ends up as an old man on the island of Patmos. It was from there that he wrote his letters. All the theological and analytical language is gone, as he repeats again and again 'Little children, let us love one another, because God has first loved us.' 'If you say you have no sin, you are a liar, and the truth is not in you, because God says that we have sinned.' 'Little children, there is a power within you that is greater than any evil power you will meet on the road of life.' John's letters are gems, and my friend had a very gentle and beautiful introduction to her reading of the Bible.

The Acts of the Apostles is a gold-mine, when we come to reflect on the church of today, and why we need that 'New Pentecost' that Blessed John XXIII prayed for. Any attempt at renewal within the church today is an attempt to return to the church that Jesus founded, the church of the early Christian community. We learn a great deal about the early church through the letters of Paul, in particular. They had their occasional row, their occasional scandal, and their occasional personality clash. It helps to 'anchor' one in the church when I look at it on a broader canvas.

For the person who has engaged in any kind of extensive Bible study, my answer to the above question will surely appear as 'Kindergarten Stuff'. I accept that totally, because I am writing here for those who have little or no knowledge of the Bible, and are certainly not familiar with using it in their everyday Christian life. This is the source of the question being posed. My answer is an attempt to encourage people to take their Bible in hand, and allow themselves be led by the Holy Spirit into the vast amount of spiritual treasures that it contains. If I get that Bible in someone's hands, my answer will have achieved what I set out to do.

What is meant by 'The Communion of Saints'?

The 'Communion of Saints' is an all-inclusive term for the church, which is made up of us here now, all those in heaven, and all the souls in purgatory. The official terms for each of these categories are: The Church Triumphant (Heaven), The Church Militant (Earth), and the Church Suffering (Purgatory). Perhaps 'the Church Militant' is too strong a term to use in these days, but it can continue to describe those of us still struggling along the way. These three groups are connected to each other, and there is plenty of scope for interplay between them.

Obviously, those in heaven can help us, and we frequently seek their help. On the other hand, we can help the souls in purgatory, and they look towards us for that help. Strange as it may seem, the souls in purgatory can help us because part of their purgatory is that they cannot help themselves, or better their condition in any way.

Looking towards the Church Triumphant has always been part of the prayer life of the church. Those who are canonised have their own feastdays, when they are given special remembrance, sometimes preceded by a Novena, when we bring our petitions to the saint and ask for an answer to our prayers. My mother and father are still my parents and, just as Jesus recognises his Mother in heaven, I expect to be able to recognise my parents. I also believe that my parents are more a power for good and for blessings in my life now than they ever could be while alive, no matter how good they were. Padre Pio and Thérèse of Lisieux, among others, said that their real work would begin after they died.

I'm not sure that this is taken seriously by many people, because all they experience in bereavement is a terrible sense of loss. This is very understandable when, for example, a young mother is left to rear a young family on her own, and all the dreams she had for the future are shattered. I suspect that this situation begins to improve largely through the help of the departed one, who is still the parent of these children, and must surely still have a responsibility towards them.

Many of our canonised saints were known to have a special devotion to a canonised saint of a previous time, e.g. the Curè of Ars and St Philomena, Thérèse of Lisieux and St Joseph, etc. Of course, I don't have to confine my prayers and my confidence to canonised saints. Anyone who is in heaven is canonised, even if not officially so by the church. I myself find it difficult any more to separate my Heavenly Mother from my earthly mother. I think of them standing on either side of me as I stand at the altar for Mass. I think of them sitting on either side of my bed as I sleep at night.

I have noticed that my awareness of the souls in purgatory has developed and grown over the years. In my earlier life, this was something that formed part of the life of the church for the month of November, and didn't get any great attention outside of that time. Visiting a grave would normally form part of going to church on Sunday morning, and I like to think that such visits were occasions for genuine prayer. Over the years, however, as friends and acquaintances passed on, I have become much more aware of the souls in purgatory, and of our responsibility to them. When it comes to the prayers for the departed in the Mass, I recite the following prayer: 'Heavenly Father, we offer you the Body and Blood of Jesus on behalf of the souls in purgatory, and we ask you to pour out upon them now the fullness of forgiveness, redemption, and salvation merited for them by Jesus on Calvary, so that many of them may now come into the fullness of your presence.'

I do not consider it coincidence, but my awareness of the souls in purgatory has become much more constant and consistent since I began reciting that prayer. I look towards them for help, and am conscious of their help on many occasions. I consider it an extraordinary privilege that we have it within our power to assist souls to complete their journey into the presence of God. On its own, this is a very real act of Christian charity, but it has the added bonus of us having friends in high places.

All four Eucharistic Prayers used in the Mass help to remind us of the extent of the church. The Great Amen at the end of these prayers is a very important part, and this is our personal agreement and acceptance of all that has gone before. It is an essential part of the ritual. This is just as important as the consecration, because, without our acquiescence, we are not personally involved in the prayer. Before saying that Amen, however, there is something important that must be included. We pray for the church, and we make specific references to the Pope, our bishop, the church on earth, the deceased members of the church, the souls in purgatory, and we pray to Mary, St Joseph, the apostles, and 'all the saints'. The Mass is the Prayer of the Church, and all of the church must be included in it. Once we have acknowledged the Communion of Saints, we can become more aware of each other, as we join in the Lord's Prayer, reach out to each other with a sign of peace, and come forward together to share in Holy Communion.

If I had the gift of mysticism, as Padre Pio had, I would be able to see all the souls that are gathered together at this Mass. On one occasion he mentioned that there were more departed souls than living people present at his Mass each morning. Jesus said that wherever two or more were gathered in his name, that he would be there in the midst of them. If Jesus is there, then you can be sure that the Trinity is present. If the Trinity is present, you can be equally sure that all of heaven is present. It is true that we are more involved with the Communion of Saints than we might normally be conscious of. There is so much to be gained from a growing awareness of the extent of the church of which we form a part.

I quote the following from a little leaflet I came across, which does not give the name of the author. 'Suppose you are most anxious to get from God some great favour, and supposing God told Michael the Archangel to gather the following into one vast cathedral: 1) All the millions of the faithful on earth, from the Pope to the youngest child. 2) All the souls in Purgatory. 3) All the millions of saints in heaven. 4) All the millions of angels as well. 5) Mary our Mother. Supposing all of this chorus joined together in praising God, and in begging his mercy. What a power this prayer would have before the throne of God!' It is sad when I consider prayer as something that *I* do, completely detached from everybody else. I am a member of a Body. When I come to pray, I should 'join in the chorus'. To be consciously aware of my membership of that vast chorus is to open my heart to the constant outpouring of the Spirit that 'drives' that church. St Paul speaks about running the race, with the crowds cheering us on from the stands. St Charles of Mount Argus (Dublin) was canonised recently, and it was very moving to see thousands of Dubliners standing in the pouring rain in St Peter's Square, giving loud and prolonged cheering and applause for the new saint. To them 'he was one of ours'!

The Holy Spirit is given to the church rather than to an individual. Being part of the Christian community involves the responsibility of acting as part of a Body, and of being accountable to the other members. Some parishes bear edifying witness to this through the active involvement of so many in ministry and service. Just as we have this responsibility to each other within the Christian community, so the three dimensions of church, heaven, purgatory, and earth, have a responsibility towards each other. Those who have already arrived in heaven must be very conscious of the fact that the other two groups are on our way to join them, when we will be together for all eternity. This bond, therefore, is very strong, and is one that will never be broken. Just as we look towards those in heaven to pour down on us that shower of roses that St Thérèse promised, so the souls in purgatory are always waiting for our prayers.

They are sometimes referred to as the poor souls. The poor are always waiting. They have to wait for hand-outs, wait for the rains to come, wait for the 'flying doctors' to come by. They are powerless to speed up this process. They have no say in what affects them. They are constantly looking towards others. If there could be sadness in heaven it could/would come from the awareness of how much I could have done to help these souls on their way to the fullness of God's vision, but failed to do so. I cannot 'compartmentalise' love; I cannot confine it to select groups, or the chosen few. When I stand at the altar for Mass, I am reminded to open my heart, and my arms out wide to embrace all of God's people.

I remember, some years ago, staying with friends of mine down the country. The children were young, and we all joined in night prayers together. One of the little girls, whose heart was as big as the great outdoors, always prayed 'for all of the people of the whole wide world'. She said this with such conviction and sincerity that I was always touched by the 'scope' of such a prayer. Many years later, I now believe that prayer resounded in heaven on those occasions.

Television may have contributed to pushing reality to the fringes of our consciousness. There is nothing that can shock us anymore. When we first saw the swollen bellies of the hungry children, with flies crawling all over their faces, we were disquieted and disturbed. Nowadays those pictures are commonplace, and may no longer shock. The picture may just remain on the screen as something that is happening 'very far away', and it really has nothing to do with us. If my heart is not moved by those pictures, surely my head should tell me that these are my brothers and sisters; these are co-inhabitants with me in this world. If the Communion of Saints means anything to me, then these children should become a cause of concern for me. One of the aid agencies in our country is called Concern, and it is a very appropriate name. I spoke in the last paragraph about not compartmentalising love. When I recite my Creed, those things I claim to believe in, I say 'I believe in the Communion of Saints.' As I write this, I find myself being challenged about the truth of that claim.

The question posed was 'What is meant by the Communion of Saints'? In summary, the answer would seem to be 'The church' ... all of the church. We speak of people today who have 'left the church'. As I write this, I could well ask myself 'Have I ever belonged in the church?' Maybe it's time for me to join the church! Certainly if it means being a fully conscious, deeply committed, fully aware member of the church, then I have to broaden my vision, remove the blinkers, and open my arms out wide. I can no longer fly solo, if God has designed that I should be part of his people, reaching out to those in glory, to those suffering, and to those still struggling.

There are times when I fantasise receiving an answer to this question from the various groups in the Communion of Saints. I have attempted to answer how I myself see it. What would the saints in glory say? 'Heaven, for us, is two-fold. We enjoy the vision of God and are filled with praise and gratitude. We are also very conscious of those who will be coming to join us. Whether in purgatory, or on earth, we see them as "not in heaven yet", but we see them as belonging here. All debts are cleared, all bills are paid, and we hope and pray that those on earth will accept the offer of God's salvation, and become part of our choir. Those still on earth quite often fail to have a keen sense of belonging, which is shared among us and, indeed, among the souls in purgatory. If there is one thing we pray for more than anything else, it is that people would have that very real sense of belonging, and that they would be deeply conscious of the Communion that binds us all together.'

The souls in Purgatory would have two ways of looking at this question. They look towards those in glory to assist them with their prayers, and to do this as part of their praise and thanks to God for his goodness to them. They look towards us for prayers, much more conscious than we are of how many blessings are available to us through our prayers for them. They long for prayers from us, both for their sakes, and for ours.

And that brings us back to us … I hope that my attempt at answering this question has helped to broaden our vision of church. I hope that it has alerted us to the need of having a sense of belonging. I hope it deepens our sense of accompaniment on our journey, as we await the Great Rendezvous around the throne of God, when we won't have to say 'goodbye' anymore.

What is '12-Step Spirituality'?

To help our understanding, it is necessary right from the start to be certain what we mean by 'Spirituality'. We are quite familiar with the word 'Religion'. It comes from the Latin word *religare*, which means *to be obliged, to be bound by*. 'Religious Life' is a life that is bound by a set of monastic rules, and has its own sets of obligations and responsibilities. Religion is something we do; it is a man/woman-made thing. It is about rules and regulations, and, fundamentally, it is about control. Religion is about externals and, without Spirituality (of which we'll speak in a moment), it has no soul, and can be very dangerous and destructive. 'Pure/fundamental' religion, i.e. divorced from spirituality, has always been destructive. There is not a war in today's world that is not a religious one, where people continue to kill each other 'in God's name'. 'Spirituality', on the other hand, is internal, it is what God does in us, and it is about *surrender*. The question is about spirituality, and the answer will be about spirituality.

12-Step Spirituality is something that was given by God to two alcoholics in 1935. I say this 'given by God' very deliberately, because I genuinely believe that no human being could have thought this up on his/her own. It is a most extraordinary programme that is so simple, so uncomplicated, and so unchanging that it just has to be from God. The men's names were Bill Wilson and Bob Smith, affectionately known as 'Bill and Bob'. Bob came from quite a religious background, but he soon discovered that, when it came to his battle with alcoholism, his religion did not seem to help at all. (Right here, let me state *why*. Religion is what we do, and there is nothing we can do that can rectify something over which we are powerless. That, in effect, belongs to the realm of Spirituality, which is something that God does.)

Bill had no religious background but, in his despair, he cried out to 'Somebody out there' ('if you're there'!). His room lit up, and he had what is called a 'religious experience'. He didn't understand what was happening, but he knew he had made contact with 'the God of the preachers'. He had his own 'Road to Damascus' experience, and he knew that he had found what he had been searching for. He discovered that he had access to a Power and, not knowing what it was, it came to be called 'God, as we understood him'. To this day, in Twelve-Step literature, God is always referred to in these words, and is equally referred to as 'The Higher Power'.

Bill stopped drinking, and he was inspired to go in search of another alcoholic with whom he could test his discovery. Bill went on business from New York to the mid-west, and he encountered Bob, a doctor, and a chronic alcoholic. He told Bob about his discovery, and they both set out to explore this new discovery. The kernel of their discovery was a) that they were powerless over alcohol, and b) that this new-found God could 'fix' their predicament, if he were allowed. When they discovered that it worked for both of them, they went in search of others to share their good news with them. Soon there were many groups of people who came to discover that God could do for them what they never could do for themselves. Today, as I write, there are millions of recovering alcoholics successfully following this simple programme in every corner of the globe.

What is this programme? Because the early members were so convinced that this was God's work, not theirs, they decided to remain anonymous, and, so, they came up with the name *Alcoholics Anonymous*. Bill wrote a book (affectionately referred as *The Big Book*), in which he recounted all their discoveries, and how the programme worked for them. The end result was the evolution of the Twelve Steps, which was presented as a programme of recovery. From the very beginning, the programme was seen as a *spiritual* programme, and they resisted all attempts by any church or religious institution to take it over, to influence it, or to control it. Its success lies in having retained that independence right down to this day.

They had Twelve Steps for recovery, and Twelve Traditions

to preserve the unity and integrity of the programme. Today, I can attend an AA meeting in any country in the world, and, apart from language difference, they are all identical. There are no 'authorities' in AA, as each group is autonomous. There are no rules, beyond the ordinary common sense requirements of behaviour that facilitate the proper running of the meeting. It does not involve itself with money, beyond a 'secret' collection at each meeting to defray expenses, e.g. hire of premises, literature, and the old reliable of tea/coffee and biscuits at the end of each meeting. The only people who are paid are a few secretaries in Head Offices who distribute literature, publish newssheets, and provide other essential services, such as telephone enquiries, convention notices, etc. The only requirement for membership is a desire to stop drinking.

What are the Twelve Steps? The first three Steps have to do with surrender. This is what ensures that it's a spiritual programme. Firstly, I have to admit that I am powerless, and my life has become unmanageable. Next I come to believe (slowly!) that a Power greater than myself can restore me to sanity. (While I may baulk at the implication of being insane, I may be realistic enough to admit that my behaviour is quite insane. Doing the same things again and again, and expecting different results each time, is insane!). Thirdly, I make a decision to turn my will and my life over to the care of God *as I understand him.* The First Step is the only one I can, and must, do 100%.

To better understand what exactly is meant by turning my will and my life over to God, one may have to go back to the first time one fell in love! Do you remember?! You may remember sublimating your owns preferences, and doing things and going places just to please the 'other'? You had no interest in football, or you were not into movies, but because you had given the other person priority in your life, you did what was pleasing to the other. If you want to know when you are doing the will of God (as you understand him!), ask yourself these simple questions: Would God approve how you treated that person this morning? ... how you spoke to that person yesterday? ... how you acted or behaved in some particular situation? If he would, then you are doing his will. Self-will run riot is what's causing your problems. By doing God's will, you are ending that insanity.

Steps Four and Five have to do with clearing the wreckage of the past. You cannot move forward freely if you are carrying burdens of sin, hurts, resentments, unforgiveness, or angers from the past. In Step Four, you list them, as you remember them. To ensure a healthy balance that avoids a guilt-trip, make sure you write down the good things as well! In Step Five you 'dump' the lot! You present your past to God, as you understand him. You ensure that you hold this mirror up to yourself, and acknowledge that this is you. Finally, you share all of that with a trusted and wise person, someone who is qualified to deal with personal sharing, either through training, or through personal experience of similar brokenness. AA is based on the principle of one alcoholic understanding and helping another, as with Bill and Bob at the very beginning.

The Sixth and Seventh Steps have to do with the shortcomings and defects of character revealed in that inventory. You make a list of these, and you'll find some or all of them in the Seven Deadly Sins, i.e., Pride, Avarice (greed, wanting the property of another), Lust, Gluttony, Envy, Anger, and Sloth (laziness). When you have identified them, you then become ready and willing for God to remove them … you ask him to do so.

The Eighth and Ninth Steps have to with making amends for all the harm your insane behaviour has done to others. Making your list is easy enough, but making amends is not so simple. Some of the people may be dead, or you don't know where they are right now. Making amends could open past wounds, or injure others in the process. As the programme suggests, you make amends 'except when to do so would injure them or others.' You wouldn't go to a person and apologise for being in an illicit relationship with that person's spouse! You should hesitate about presenting your boss with your embezzlement, as this may cost you your job, and adversely affect your family. There are many different ways of making amends, and you should seek advice on this, possibly from the person with whom you shared your Fifth Step. One of the many problems that can arise is what to do if the person refuses to accept your attempt at making amends.

And now we come to The Programme! While we will always have to do the first three steps (lest we forget!), the actual programme is Steps Ten, Eleven, and Twelve. In Step Ten, we do a daily inventory, and when we are wrong, we promptly admit it. (There would never be a war, if somebody somewhere was prepared to say 'I'm sorry, I was wrong.') In Step Eleven we seek through prayer to deepen our conscious contact with God (as we understand him!), seeking only for knowledge of his will for us, and the power to carry that out. Note well the opening words of Step Twelve: *Having had a spiritual awakening as a result of these Steps* … There is nothing haphazard here; the spiritual awakening is to be expected. Because of that spiritual awakening, we try to bring this message to others (as Bill did), and to practise these Steps in everything we do. Which brings us to the broader picture.

Up till now I have been speaking about the alcoholic. These Steps are now being used by people with addictions and compulsions of every kind. There is Drug Addicts Anonymous, Gamblers Anonymous, Sex/Love Addicts Anonymous, Overeaters Anonymous, etc. The Programme works equally well for all. The kernel of what I want to say in this answer is that I honestly believe that everyone of us could benefit enormously from following and living a Twelve-Step programme. I myself gave an eight-day Retreat to a community of enclosed Carmelite nuns on the Big Book of AA! We just replaced the word 'alcohol' by the word 'life' and moved ahead from there. We all have our demons.

I was excited by the thought of this question because it asked about *12-Step Spirituality*. It was the 'spirituality' part that excited me, because I welcome each and every opportunity I get to lead people from the controlling restrictions of religion to the liberating freedom of spirituality. Once again, I state that spirituality is internal, it's what God does, and it's about *surrender*. You can't go too far wrong there. Members of Twelve-Step programmes are not necessarily religious or church-going people. However, I cannot deny that some of the most spirit-filled people I have ever met have been at Twelve-Step meetings. One woman put it well when she said, 'The religion I got in school was to keep me from going to hell. I ended up in hell, and it was Twelve-Step Spirituality that brought me back!'

All I am hoping to do here is to answer an honest and good question. I am not 'selling' anything! If the reader is interested, and would like to enquire further, I will be very pleased indeed. I personally find the Twelve-Step Programme a source of extra-ordinary graces and blessings for me, and the only addiction I have is work! It is good to have some blue-print for living.

Anyone who has read this book up to here, or any of my other books, indeed, will know the constant stress I place on the centrality of the Spirit in the life of a Christian. From its very inception, the Twelve-Step Programme has been the work of God's Spirit. There is a wisdom in the *Big Book* that is definitely of the Spirit. All the gifts of the Spirit are to be found in this programme.

A friend of mine, a taxi driver, spent several years sleeping rough on the streets and back alleys of Dublin. I often gave him a mug of tea and a few sandwiches at the side door. The last time I met him I was sitting mesmerised as I listened to him give a talk on prayer and meditation at a meeting. Another friend lost everything through alcohol … wife, kids, home, job, dignity, etc. One day he was sitting on the kerb (unable to stand!) in the rain, with an old coat tied with a rope, wild beard, and fuzzy dirty hair that stood out like a furze bush. He held out a hand towards the passers-by, and one young woman put a coin on his hand. He looked and saw that it was his own daughter, and she didn't recognise him. That was 'Skid Row' for him! He couldn't stand up, and he was speechless. He crawled on all fours over to the corner of a side lane, fell on his face in the rain, and cried out to God to help him. That was 42 years ago, and Gerry hasn't had a drink since. The miracle of Bill Wilson continues.

I would not wish, gentle reader, to leave you with the impression that you have to end up on Skid Row before you have a spiritual awakening! What I have written in this answer is intended for those who are entirely unaware that they may need a spiritual awakening, because they may not have any real struggle in their lives, and they may be living a life-giving religious life. I present this answer in the hope that even the general approach to God and to life that this programme advocates might appeal to as many people as possible. There is a whole library on Twelve-Step living available, and any of us could benefit even from reading one of those books. (Yes, I have written one, *Simple Steps to Spiritual Living*.) For someone who is actively involved in this programme, what I have written may come across as simplistic, and kindergarten stuff. I have no problem with that, because all I hope to offer is a 'starter-kit' that may lead the reader to other things. My purpose was to answer the question posed. Anything else is a bonus.

Tell me about Charismatic Renewal

'Charism' means a gift, but a very special kind of gift. It is a gift that is given us for the benefit of others. They could be called 'service gifts' because, even if it is we who use them, it is others who should benefit from them. Examples of such gifts are healing, teaching, preaching, etc. Most gifts could actually be accepted as charismatic because, effectively, God doesn't give me anything for myself. (He doesn't give me my gift of speech to go around talking to myself!) When the Holy Spirit comes (Pentecost), he brings all the gifts with him. He comes 'to complete Jesus' work on earth', but he does that through us. In simple words, he comes and he brings the complete 'toolbox' with him. Depending on the work he is doing through us, he supplies the gifts of Wisdom, Discernment, Knowledge, Faith, Prophecy, etc. He never asks us to do anything without giving us the gift we need to do that. It is God's work, so God supplies the power. 'The kingdom, the power, and the glory are yours'. If I supply any of the power I may be tempted to steal some of the glory.

'Charismatic Renewal' is an unfortunate choice of title, because it can be misleading. It stresses the charisms, or the gifts, and, of course, *all renewal* is about the Spirit. Despite this misnomer, I can continue to answer the question about Charismatic Renewal, as long as it is kept in proper perspective. The charisms do play an important part, of course, but if I am open to receiving the Giver (Spirit), I will, of course, receive all the gifts.

To understand the broader picture, it is necessary to return to the beginnings of the church. The prophet Isaiah said that the Messiah would be recognised by the 'signs and wonders' that would accompany him, and show that he was from God. When Jesus came, John the Baptist sent some disciples to Jesus to ask him if he were the Messiah, or should they look for another. Jesus answered, 'Look around and see for yourselves. The blind can see, the lame can walk, and the poor have good news preached to them.' In other words, look at the proofs for yourselves, and see if I am the one who was promised. When Jesus sent his apostles out to preach, he told them 'These are the signs that will accompany those who believe in me ... they will be accompanied by signs and wonders ... they shall lay their hands on the sick, and they shall be healed.' Signs and wonders were an everyday part of life in the early church. Unfortunately, these began to be neglected, and it came to be accepted that they were just intended as a help to get the early church off the ground! Signs and wonders, and special gifts, came to be seen as the preserve of the saints, and those through whom those gifts were most evident often ended up canonised! The 'charismatic dimension' of church belonged to a very exclusive club. In general, it could be said that the Divine Initiative was turned into Human Endeavour! The Holy Spirit became marginalised, if not completely neglected, and came to be known as 'The Holy Ghost'!

Vatican II was an attempt to return to our roots. In *The Church in the Modern World* we read: 'The charisms of the Spirit ought to be eagerly sought after by all of God's people, as being necessary and essential for the renewal of his Body, the church.' Unfortunately, this statement has not yet come to the foreground, and gained the prominence that is needed. There will be no effective renewal of the church until this has happened. The Lord never withdraws any of the charisms, even when they lie neglected and unused.

For example, Religious Life, as we knew it, is finished, as the schools and the convents are closing or being passed on into the hands of others. Religious Life, however, is a charism, and will always be there ... even now, as we experiment with new and different ways in which to live it. The Brothers and Sisters who conducted our Catholic schools belong to a fairly recent phenomenon of 200 years ago. One can travel the country now, and see the ruins of monasteries that dot the landscape as evidence of a former expression of the charism of Religious Life. We can live with the expectation that, one hundred years from now, we will have a form of Religious Life just as effective as anything we've ever had. We have to wait for that, however, because we don't yet know what form that living will take. The important thing to stress is that the charism is still there for the church.

Let me continue in that vein for a while. All of the charisms of the Spirit are still alive and well in the church. Maybe 'alive and well' is an unfortunate choice of words, because many of them could still be quite dormant. However, we have begun the process of rediscovery, and we can trust the Spirit to complete the work he has begun. The 'New Pentecost' for which John XXIII prayed is emerging, slowly but surely.

What we know as 'Charismatic Renewal' has been a wonderful and generous response to the rediscovery of these gifts. I said that the title may be misleading, but that is a very minor problem. Wonderful and great things have already happened to God's people over the past forty years of Charismatic Renewal. The first thing to do is to 'collect the bodies' (!), just as the apostles gathered in the Upper Room. A group of people are brought together by the Spirit, and they form a Prayer Group. Their purpose for coming together is to praise God, and to build each other up. How this happens is not really the important thing. There is one condition, however, which is of vital importance. They must discover and use all the charisms that are certainly among that group. This requires discernment and wisdom (which are charisms in themselves). If I were to stand in front of that Group, I could address them in something like the following words: 'When you make yourselves available to the Holy Spirit, you actually become the Body of Christ. You show up, provide the body, and the Spirit does all the rest. All the gifts of the Spirit are among you right now, but we may not yet know where they are, and how to discover them. Take your time, and all of that will be revealed in time. Some of you will be seen to emerge with leadership skills. Please note that this is something that others will discover, and call on you ... not something that you yourself discover! Such a person is dangerous! Someone else will be discovered to have a great gift for teaching, and will be called on by the group to exercise that gift. Yet another will utter words that are truly inspired, and we will have discovered, or uncovered, the gift of prophecy. There may be someone in the group that you'd like to go to, to be prayed with, and that person may well have the gift of healing. Don't worry ... *all* the gifts of the Spirit will emerge in time. Only then can we call this a Charismatic group, because use of the charisms plays a large part in it. It is an extraordinary privilege to be able to witness the Spirit at work among a group of people. As I said in an answer about Pentecost, it is important to remember that the Spirit is given to the Body, not to the individual.' (I had forgotten that I was still speaking to the group, and so I'd better stop!)

Forming a Prayer Group has many advantages. Most parishes are too widespread and unwieldly to be dealt with as a community. In practice, the parish may be a community of communities. It is made up of all the various groups that meet during the week, be that a Prayer Group, Bible Study Group, SVP, Legion of Mary, Divine Mercy, etc. I would even include all the young mothers who meet at the local crèche each morning. Parishioners should be strongly encouraged to attach themselves to one of these Groups. Any attempt within the parish to discover and exercise the charisms has some chance of being successful if this call is made within the smaller group. The worshipping community on a Sunday is greatly enriched if all of these streams of life come flowing into it.

For the purpose of answering the question posed, I must return to speaking about Charismatic Renewal. Despite the statement already quoted from *The Church in the Modern World*, it has been a sad fact of life that Charismatic Renewal has been more or less some sort of underground movement in some of our parishes. There is no point in getting into the blame game here, because when a Prayer Group fails to get the support and approval of local clergy, it is really everybody's fault. The blame can reach from the priest who is afraid of losing his grip on control and authority, to the 'charismaniacs' who are more filled with their own 'high spirits' than with the Spirit of God. The sad part about all this is that Satan is the one who gains when division occurs. He thrives on division, confusion, and confrontation. When this happens, the gifts of wisdom, discernment, and knowledge, among others, are being completely neglected. If there is a group in such a parish, it can scarcely be called a Charismatic Group. Having access to the gifts of the Spirit is another way of speaking about working with the power of the Holy Spirit. One thing we must never forget: The church to which we belong is the same church that was founded on that first Pentecost Sunday. The only thing that has changed is our perception of it. I well remember how impressed I was the first time I read the Acts of the Apostles, when I envied them the power and the gifts they exercised and experienced. That impression is re-ignited in 'this our day', when I consider the possibility and the availability of a return to that Pentecost.

Let me return to the title 'Charismatic Renewal' once again. I already said it was a misnomer, and now I say that, if it involves the charisms, then the word 'Renewal' is superfluous. If the gifts are being activated, then renewal is automatic … renewal is what happens. This renewal is on-going, as we continue 'to live and to walk' in the power of the Spirit.

The church must be constantly renewed 'until Christ is formed within us'. This is an extraordinary privilege, and it is happening in these, our days. In answer to another question, I suggested that God, in his infinite wisdom, has chosen these days as being the best possible days for us to be on this earth, and in this church.

In the next question, I will have an opportunity to share what hope I have for the church in these times. What I am writing now is part of that answer, of course, but there is so much more. Just as what I wrote about '12-Step Spirituality', so do I repeat here that I am not asking everybody to join! In the gospels, one man met Jesus when he got down from a sycamore tree, while another met him after being lowered on a stretcher through a roof. It matters not how it happens, as long as they met Jesus.

There are horses for courses, and any one of these 'fellowships' is more suitable to some people than to others. All I ask is that we should not have all those 'no-go' areas in our lives, without a critical examination of what is involved. I may not go to a Charismatic Renewal Prayer Group, but it certainly would be unwise and ill-advised of me to sit in judgement on those who do. Once again, we have the conflict between religion and spirituality. Religious people can never understand spiritual people. On the morning of Pentecost, Jerusalem was filled with pilgrims from all parts of the then-known world. These were religious people, probably very good people. However, once they met the apostles as they emerged from that Upper Room, their first opinion was 'These men are drunk'! Not much has changed down the years. Those who attend Charismatic Prayer Meetings are used to the jibes and the dismissive remarks of people who would consider themselves religious. 'Live, and let live' is a very wise slogan that applies to many areas of living.

One of the dimensions of Charismatic Renewal is what is called *The Life in the Spirit Seminars*. This consists of seven talks which comprise the heart of the Christian message, and it involves the opportunity for a Pentecost experience. The talks are simple, and very basic, and take place over a seven-week period. There is a logical sequence to the talks, as each one flows out of the previous one. The first has to do with God's love, and his plan in Creation. The second has to do with how we messed up that plan through Original Sin, and how we became so damaged that we were in need of being recreated. The third is about Jesus coming to set things right again, and enable us return to a Garden-relationship with God. The fourth tells about how the Spirit took over from Jesus, to complete his work. The fifth teaches us how to pray for that Spirit, and it helps us have an 'Upper Room' attitude to enable us experience Pentecost. The sixth is about living and walking in the power of that Spirit. And, finally, the seventh talk speaks about the transformed lives that result from all of the above.

This is pure evangelism ... indeed it is one of the few specific examples of evangelising that is evident in the church. While I hesitate to suggest that everyone should attend Charismatic Prayer Meetings, I would dearly long to see the day when every-one would do a *Life in the Spirit Seminar*. This can be done com-pletely independent of Charismatic Renewal, with the exact same effect. Within the past two years I have been involved in giving some of these talks, and in two areas, I gave all seven talks, without using one Charismatic expression! Some of those present might not be keen on attending, if they thought 'this is Charismatic' (!), so I omitted anything that could be identified as being specifically Charismatic, and all was well. While this was an exhilarating experience, it was also tinged with sadness, when I thought that every parish in the country could have this Pentecost experience, if there was enough goodwill.

'The Company of Believers', as the early Christian communi-ties were called, were a complete mystery to those who watched them in action. This was something new indeed, and it was diffi-cult to understand. However, there was one thing that was no-ticed, and could not be denied. 'See how these Christians love one another.' The greatest gift of all is *love*. Members of a Prayer Group need never be confused, afraid, or discouraged, if they put *love* at the very top of their agenda. The presence of real love is something that cannot be denied, even by the most sceptical of critics. 'Where there is love, there is God … *Ubi caritas, ibi Deus est.*' The surest way of having the gifts is to stress the greatest gift of all. The Spirit is the expressed love of the Father and the Son, the very breath and power of God. It's just a question of get-ting our priorities right, and of keeping them right. After that we can't go too far astray.

What hope can you have for the church?

I hesitated to take this question on its own, because, between my answers about Pentecost and Charismatic Renewal, I may already have dealt with much of what I'd have to say here. However, upon reflection, I feel that this question requires its own treatment, without necessarily repeating much of what has gone before.

At the very beginning, let me say with total emphasis that my hope is based on the life, death, teachings, and promises of Jesus. This is his church, and from the turbulence and travail of Calvary to this very day, it is under constant attack from the evil one. And yet Jesus tells us, 'The gates of hell will not prevail against it.' The church reminds me of those trick candles that are often put on a child's birthday cake. Every time the child blows out the candles, they just light up again!

My mother never lit a fire in the winter. At night-time she got a bucket of turf-mould, dampened it, and packed the stove with it, ensuring that all draught vents were closed. The following morning she opened up the front of the stove, got a poker, and rattled down all the ashes. And there, of course, were the red hot coals which had survived the night. A few sods of turf on top of that, and we were off for the day! Over the latter part of my lifetime, the church has been in the business of rattling down all the ashes, and exposing the hot coals that are never extinguished. When I read Pope Benedict's first letter, *God is Love*, I thought of it as recovering the hot coals again.

Jesus entrusted his church to the Holy Spirit and to his Mother. It was this combination of the Spirit and Mary that made Jesus present in human form in the first place. St Paul never actually met Jesus. He was persecuting the followers of Jesus, when he was knocked off his horse on the way to Damascus. 'Saul, Saul. Why are you persecuting me?' a voice asked him. 'Who are you, Lord?' Paul asked him. 'I am Jesus whom you are persecuting', came the reply. From that moment, Paul made no distinction between Jesus, and his Body, the church. The church was Jesus made present in another form. The original body of Christ was nailed to a cross on Calvary, and breathed forth its last breath there. As we know, of course, that was not the end. There have been many times since, when to human eyes it appeared that the Body of Christ was finished, but such occasions continued to be followed by yet another Easter. If I had stood at the foot of the cross with Mary on Calvary, she would have spoken to me about an Easter that was only around the corner. That, in essence, gentle reader, is what gives me the hope that I have for the church. Jesus died once, and he will never die again.

The church was, effectively, wiped out in France during the French Revolution. Napoleon threatened to stable his horses in the Vatican. Stalin and Chairman Mao eliminated all religious practices from within their dominions. And yet, of course, as we all know, all these self-appointed deities have been shown to have had feet of clay, and the church continues to speak the gospel message to the world. It was significant, only last year, that Mother Teresa's Sisters were invited to come and work in China. Blessed Mother Teresa always had the ambition of bringing her Sisters to China, but she had to die and return to the throne of God before that could be effected.

When we speak of the church we are speaking about an on-going Easter. People who do not understand this simple truth are the ones who speak of the death of the church in these our days, while those of us in the church realise with great joy that we are witnessing the birth of a whole new church.

Jesus neither demanded nor expected perfection from his apostles. Rather did he hope that they would be convinced and convicted of their human weakness, so as to be open to the power of the Spirit that he would send to them. Grace builds on nature, rather than replacing it. Even after Pentecost, we read of several upsets, disputes, and differences of opinion among the early Christian community. Paul went up to Jerusalem to confront Peter. Paul parted company with Mark because of a clash of personalities. There were heated arguments for and against compulsory circumcision, which was amicably resolved. Nothing much has changed in the church down the years! The human dimension will always be there, while the Spirit continues to write straight on crooked lines.

It is absolutely essential for us to remember the divine origin and purpose of the church, and the constant guidance of the Holy Spirit in the on-going life of the church. Otherwise, we could easily lose our nerve, our hope, and even our faith. There were many good bishops who travelled to attend the Vatican II Council, quite convinced that all was well with the church. Their tunnel-vision prevented them seeing what the Spirit clearly saw, i.e. that the church had become like the valley of dry bones that confronted Ezekiel in the desert. The church was badly in need of an overhaul, and Pope John XXIII was the least likely person to effect such a task. Once again, the Spirit took back control of the church, and we are still in the throes of the rebirth that emerged from that Council.

These are exciting times. Not only am I hopeful, but I am genuinely grateful to be alive during this era in the life of the church. I have long ago ceased to try and second-guess the Spirit as to what is likely to happen next, because I am totally confident that the church is in safe hands. In recent years when we have been bedevilled by scandals, and the media are having a field day at the expense of the church, it is very important to remember that 'This too will pass'. We have been here before, on various other issues, when the media were happy to consign the church to the death columns. Time and again, however, Jesus was awakened in the boat, and he stood up, and 'rebuked the wind and the seas, and there came a calm'. When all the present-day scribblers and TV chat-show hosts are dead and buried, the church will continue to repent, to be renewed, and to proclaim the gospel of Jesus. I am not afraid of scandals, even though I abhor the evil that is effected on the innocent, and I condemn all such abominations. When I say that I am not afraid of scandals, what I mean is that I *want* all scandals to be exposed, no matter how shocking, no matter how ugly. The Spirit of Truth cannot build on deceit and cover-up. I want all the scandals in the cupboard to be hung out in full view, so that we can be exorcised of all such evils. Not, of course, that we can hope the evils will all end. While we are human, we will always witness the ugly side of our humanity. What I pray for is that the church will never again provide protection and cover-up for something that is inherently wrong. We should never be afraid of the truth, because, as Jesus tells us, only the truth will set us free.

Another reason for the hope that I have is the great love and esteem I have for our pope, Pope Benedict XVI. Pope John Paul II was a hard act to follow. However, by now it must be obvious to all who care to know, that the Lord provides the leader that is needed at any one time. John Paul II applied the brakes to a 'runaway church' in some parts of the world. Without a bullet or a bomb, he took on the might of Communism, and contributed to the symbolic collapse of the Berlin Wall. Each pope brings his own unique charism to the office. Pope Benedict is a humble, gentle, loving shepherd, who invites and calls, rather than confronts. He did the confronting very effectively when he was entrusted with the role of protector of the church's teachings in his last post. That particular role prevented most of us from getting to know the real person behind the role. From the moment of his election as Pope he has opened his arms to the world. He has extended the hand of friendship to other churches and, in his latest book, he has invited us to return to the Jesus of the gospels. 'An "adult" faith is not a faith that follows the trends of fashion, and the latest novelty; a mature adult faith is deeply rooted in Christ … Truth and love coincide in Christ. To the extent that we draw close to Christ, in our own lives too, truth and love are blended. Love without truth would be blind; truth without love would be like a "clanging cymbal"'(Homily prior to Conclave). His first letter was *God is Love*, which tells us a great deal about his thinking and attitude. Rather than being the 'Vatican Rottweiler' of the tabloids, I prefer to think of him as the German Shepherd of his flock! He was eighty on his last birthday, so, as he himself says, no one knows how much time or health he may have left. That is why, with typical humility and honesty, he published the first ten chapters of his book recently and, if the Lord gives him enough health and time, he will finish it in due course! In his famous statement of his own personal beliefs (*Crossing the Threshold of Hope*) Pope John Paul II repeated again and again 'Be not afraid.' After his election Pope Benedict spoke these words to the cardinals: 'In my soul there are two contrasting sentiments in these hours. On the one hand, a sense of inadequacy and human turmoil for the responsibility entrusted to me yesterday as the Successor of the Apostle Peter in this See of Rome, with regard to the universal church. On the other hand, I sense within me profound gratitude to God who does not abandon his flock, but leads it throughout time, under the guidance of those he has chosen as vicars of his Son. This intimate recognition for a gift of divine mercy prevails in my heart in spite of everything. I consider this a grace obtained for me by my venerated predecessor, John Paul II. It seems I can feel his strong hand squeezing mine; I seem to see his smiling eyes, and listen to his words, addressed to me especially at this moment: "Do not be afraid".' I am strongly resisting the temptation to quote more and more of his beautiful words on many many occasions. However, what I have quoted will help give some insight into the wonderful personality of the man. Yes, indeed, he is one of the special reasons I have for the hope that is mine for the church today.

I look back with gratitude and amazement at all the changes that have taken place in the church during my lifetime. We are slowly, but surely, making our way back over the bridge again from the love of law to the law of love. I remember rattling off my list of 'sins' at my First Confession. Children of today would not be allowed use such language. Rather they speak about 'spoiling love' when they failed to do what they knew to be right. They speak about love, rather than about sin. While there will always be personal wrong-doing, there is a greater emphasis today on communal sin, on the sins of injustice perpetrated by

one nation against another, by one group of people against another. Half the world is dying of hunger, while the other half
goes on diets to correct the modern scourge of obesity. Ethnic
cleansing, which has become an ugly feature of today's world, is
a crime crying out to God for justice. The monopoly of power
and riches in the hands of a few, while the vast majority of God's
people cannot enjoy basic human rights, is something that the
church today continues to highlight.

Unfortunately, in the past, in places like Latin America, the
church was seen to be on the side of the conqueror and the
colonialist. Many of our courageous leaders (Romero) have paid
with their lives by challenging the powers-that-be, and speaking
out on behalf of the voiceless. The church must always speak
with a prophetic voice, condemning the evils of the age.
Prophets have often ended up as martyrs, because the messenger gets shot when the listeners don't like the message. It is in
this context that we are told 'Be not afraid'. Jesus tells us that we
can expect the world to treat us as it treated him.

One of the most amazing experiences of recent times was the
worldwide attention given to the dying and death of Pope John
Paul II. It was amazing, because it was so unusual. The leopard
doesn't change its spots, of course, so in a way that was but a
seven-day wonder. It was impressive and encouraging, however,
because it showed that even a secularist/materialistic world
cannot but be moved by a voice that speaks with courageous
love. Mother Teresa received the love and attention of all religions and of none. All of this shows that the voice of the church
can still be heard amidst the din of the marketplace.

I began this answer by saying that my hope for the church lay
in the life, death, resurrection, teachings, and promises of Jesus
Christ. That, of course, is the source of my greatest hope. The
church, the Body of Christ, has been on Calvary on many occasions throughout history. One of the saddest elements during
the most recent of those dark times was that some members of
the church began to lose hope. Losing hope is one of the few sins
that a Christian can commit. The word 'hope' is not used in the

gospels, but it constantly occurs in the post-Easter/Pentecost writings of the New Testament. Calvary leading to Easter is a journey of hope. Death is the 'final enemy', and Jesus has overcome that. If we can overcome death itself, then there's nothing in life that cannot be overcome.

We are a resurrected people, who already have the victory. The decisive battle has been fought and won. We need never fear those who can destroy the body, but those who can destroy the soul as well. In Jesus is our victory; in Jesus is our hope. Jesus is the victor who can never become the vanquished. The church is the Body of Christ, which is a risen body. In earlier times, when a country was invaded, and the enemy driven back out again, heralds were sent to the main cities to *proclaim* that victory. The people gathered in the town square to hear the herald proclaim the Good News. That is what the gospel is, and it is that victory that we are asked to proclaim in every town and village and parish. Our message is one of victory, of Good News, of sure and certain *hope*.

What do you mean by 'Divine Mercy devotion'?

I will begin with a brief history of this devotion, relative to who received the message, what that message was, and how it was received and spread. Helena Kowalska was born in Poland in 1905. When she was twenty years old, she entered the Congregation of the Sisters of Our Lady of Mercy, and from then on she was known as Sister Faustina. She lived there for thirteen years, before her death at the early age of thirty-three. She had a deep personal devotion to Jesus, with trust in his Divine Mercy, which she endeavoured to instil into everyone who came to know her. In 1931, when she was 26 years old, she received the first part of the message. 'I saw Jesus dressed in a white garment. He held one hand raised in blessing, and the other hand was touching his garment at the breast. From under the garment came two rays of light, one red, the other pale.' Jesus asked her to paint a picture of what she saw, with the words *Jesus I trust in You* written below the picture. He asked that this picture be venerated, first in her chapel, and then throughout the world. Jesus explained the significance of the rays. 'The rays represent the Blood and Water which gushed forth from the depths of my mercy when my agonising heart was pierced on the cross. The pale rays symbolise the water, which cleanses and purifies the soul; the red rays represent the blood, which gives new life to the soul.'

Because I am anxious to get on to the actual devotion itself, I will just briefly summarise what happened since that first message until the Feast of Divine Mercy was officially established in the church, and Faustina was canonised a saint. The message met with the usual responses from both enthusiasts and doubters. The whole project was tested, when inaccurate reports arrived in Rome, causing promotion of this devotion to be banned. This was part of Faustina's trials, as she died before the devotion received official church approval. This untruth was soon revealed, and the ban was lifted. It is interesting to note that the one person who did most to straighten out this misunderstanding was the local Cardinal in Poland, later to become Pope John Paul II. He was a fervent apostle and devotee of this devotion from the beginning, and he had the unique honour of establishing the Sunday after Easter as the universal Feast of Divine Mercy for the whole church. He followed this by the canonisation of Saint Faustina in the year 2000.

In a previous chapter, I spoke of Charismatic Renewal being a sort of underground movement in some parishes, where those involved feel that they are merely being tolerated by the official church. Divine Mercy, on the other hand, has been publicly established, approved, and promoted by the official church, given its own specific Feastday, and incorporated into the heart of the church's teaching. With the establishment of the Feastday, and the canonisation of St Faustina, we can move confidently ahead, and give this devotion our full acceptance, and total involvement.

On a personal note, I smiled as I wrote the above paragraph, because of memories I have of my mother. As long as I can remember this picture hung above her bed. During the twenty years when the devotion was without church approval, she resolutely refused to move that picture. When the devotion was finally reinstated it was like a personal vindication for her! Up to the time of her death, she would point out that picture to visitors, and tell them that she knew the devotion would be sanctioned, and she remained loyal to it, 'in spite of dungeon, fire and sword'! (I can imagine her now, smiling and nodding her head as I write these words!)

What is this devotion? The message of Divine Mercy is at the heart of the gospel. It presents the truth and the call of the gospel, and is proclaimed by Pope John Paul II, in his encyclical *Rich in Mercy* as a message from God for our times: 'The church must consider it one of her principal duties – at every stage of history, and especially in our modern age … to proclaim and to introduce into life the mystery of Divine Mercy, supremely revealed in Jesus Christ on the cross. Over and over again, Our Lord expressed his desire to Saint Faustina that the whole world be convinced of his mercy, and he promised to defend throughout their lives those who would proclaim his mercy.'

I draw attention to the words of the Pope 'as a message of God for our times'. This is very important, and it must be stressed. It is said that 'where sin abounds, there grace abounds much more'. Our world today is greatly in need of an outpouring of Divine Mercy. The world is like a wounded stag, that stubbornly fights on to its own destruction. There is a sense of 'precipice living' in today's world. Not only are we destroying each other, but we are slowly destroying the world in which we live. Humankind is sick, and seems to have lost its compassion. I am far from being without hope, but I must be realistic and describe things as they are.

There is a story in the Old Testament of the prophet who begged God to have mercy on his people. God told him that if he found one hundred good men in the city, he would not destroy it. It seems the prophet checked, and returned to the Lord with the plea, 'Lord, will you spare the city if I find fifty good men there?' God promised to spare the city. The numbers dropped to forty, to thirty, to twenty. I refer to that here, as I imagine what a powerful miracle would be witnessed by the whole world, if every man, woman, and child on earth fell on their knees, and asked for God's mercy. I know well that that is too much to hope for, but I also know that the very idea should spur me on to inspire as many as I possibly can to fall on their knees on behalf of the others.

The Devotion is called 'Divine Mercy', but it could also be called The Divine Amnesty. God is offering the hand of friendship and the hug of reconciliation. There is nobody outside of this circle. Again and again, Jesus repeats to Faustina 'The greater the sinner, the greater the mercy. The well of Mercy was opened wide with a lance on the cross, for all souls. I do not exclude anyone. Tell ailing mankind to draw close to my Merciful Heart, and I will fill them with peace. Mankind will not find solace until it turns with confidence to my Mercy and Love.' Before going on to the prayers that form part of this Devotion, I want to stress that this is an offer of a Divine Amnesty to the people in today's world. This is a time of extraordinary outpouring of God's love and forgiveness. The Novena that precedes the Feast, and which begins on Good Friday, is a most extraordinary grace. When accompanied by certain simple conditions (Confession, Holy Communion), we obtain a complete remission of all sin, and all punishment. In Old Testament times, they had the Year of Atonement, which occurred every five years, during which all debts were cancelled, and all sins were forgiven. This Novena of Divine Mercy is surely a Divine Amnesty.

The Feast of Divine Mercy is now an official church feast. It is sad, therefore, that it still has not been given universal recognition in the church. The selection of this Sunday, as well as the distinct desire of Jesus that priests preach sermons on this day about Divine Mercy, is something that cannot be taken lightly. Jesus devoted fourteen revelations to the establishment of this Feast.

We sin 'in what we do, and in what we fail to do'. It sometimes appears that the more generous God becomes, the more we build barriers to his love. It is as if we are unwilling to be 'bought over; we'd rather pay for our own lunch, thank you'! Pride, which was at the heart of Original Sin, is still very much alive and well within the human psyche. No matter how we approach the Lord, or no matter what form of devotion we use, our approach must be one based on knowing our place before God. He is the Creator, and we are the creatures. He is the Saviour and we are the sinners. He is immortal and infinite, and we are very mortal, and very finite. It is not possible to exaggerate the chasm between God and us, one that can only be bridged by God himself. Jesus and the Spirit form the two arms of God, stretched out to embrace us, and draw us to the Father. It is not possible for us to return to the Garden on our own. Jesus is our 'Bridge over Troubled Waters', and unless we cross by using that bridge, we drown. Original Sin is no longer original. Adam and Eve decided to do it their way, and we can still persist in this stubbornness. Jesus obviously is making a distinct connection between the Paschal Mystery of our redemption, that culminated with Easter, and the feast of Divine Mercy on the very next Sunday. It is designed for the purpose that we contemplate on that day the mystery of redemption as the greatest revelation of Divine Mercy towards us. It is indeed very appropriate that, after the supreme sacrifice of Calvary, and the glorious victory of Easter, we should follow with a special celebration of the outpouring of Divine Mercy that flows from all of that.

The central prayer of this devotion is known as the *Chaplet*. It can be used with the aid of a Rosary beads. We begin with the Creed, the Our Father, and the Hail Mary. Each 'decade' begins with the prayer: 'Eternal Father, we offer you the Body and Blood, soul and Divinity of your dearly beloved Son, our Lord Jesus Christ, in atonement for our sins, and for the sins of the whole world.' On the following ten beads we recite: 'For the sake of his sorrowful Passion, have mercy on us and on the whole world.' At the end of the fifth decade we recite three times: 'Holy God, Holy Mighty One, Holy Immortal One, have mercy on us and on the whole world.' That's it! Short and simple. Reciting this Chaplet each day constitutes the Novena, which begins on Good Friday and finishes on the Sunday after Easter (which we must insist on calling *The Feast of Divine Mercy*). If we use the name often enough it may eventually attain universal usage.

Another dimension of this devotion is what is called *The Hour of Great Mercy*. This is at three o' clock in the afternoon, to coincide with the time that Jesus died. Jesus said to Saint Faustina, 'At three o' clock implore my Mercy especially for sinners and, if only for a few moments, immerse yourself in my Passion, particularly in my abandonment at the moment of agony. This is the hour of great Mercy for the whole world. At this hour I will refuse nothing to the soul that makes a request of me in virtue of my Passion. At this hour you can obtain anything for yourself, and for others, for the asking; it was the time of grace for the whole world, the moment when Mercy triumphed over Justice.' The prayers that form part of the three o'clock devotions are: 'You expired, Jesus, but the source of Life gushed forth for souls, and an ocean of Mercy opened up for the whole world. O Fount of Life, unfathomable Divine Mercy, envelop the whole world, and empty yourself out upon us.' The following prayer is generally added to the above: 'O Blood and Water, which gushed forth from the heart of Jesus as a fount of Mercy for us, I trust in you.'

The work of God's Spirit involves revealing God's love and our own sinfulness to us. In doing this, the Spirit is called the Spirit of Truth, because the extent of God's love and the depth of our sinfulness are two truths on which the Spirit can build. It is only this truth that will set us free. This devotion is based on these two basic truths. I know that it is not possible for the human mind to comprehend the extent of God's love, or our own sinfulness, but I have no doubt that if I could I would embrace the grace of Divine Mercy with open arms, and a grateful heart. 'What more can I do for my people that I have not done?' cries the Lord through the prophet Isaiah. I asked my God how much he loved me, and he stretched both arms out fully and said 'This much', and then he died. 'Greater love than this no one has ...'

In Creation, God opened out an era of great love. In these our days, he is opening up an era of infinite mercy. It is not unreasonable to expect that this could be followed by an era of infinite justice. When Sodom and Gomorrah refused to listen, when the words of the prophets go unheeded, it is reasonable to presume that mankind will have passed judgement on itself, and because of the centrality of freewill, it will have put itself outside the control of God's loving forgiveness. In his letter to the Romans, St Paul says that our salvation is based 'on his blood, and on our faith'. There is nothing automatic about God. Jesus offers, but we must accept. Jesus does not give me anything; rather he offers me everything.

From answers given to other questions in this book, it must

be obvious that the Spirit is at the heart of all of God's actions in our lives. Of ourselves, we can neither discover nor respond. Once again, when we speak of the Divine Mercy, we recall the words of Jesus to Peter, 'You are a happy man, Simon, because flesh and blood has not revealed this to you, but my Father who is in heaven.' There is little point in 'pushing' or trying to 'sell' this devotion, because it is only the Spirit who can enlighten the heart with faith.

The word 'trust' figures largely in this devotion, and trust is something that comes only after a certain time of personal experience. When I am brought from knowing *about* Jesus' love, and from knowing *about* my own sinfulness, to the point when I can claim to personally *know* both of those truths, then I am ready to open my heart to the graces of this devotion. Both truths are ideal for inculcating humility, and humility is a basic requirement for being open to these graces. Not much point in speaking about forgiveness to someone who is not convinced that she is in need of it.

I have enjoyed writing these reflections, because I happen to be deeply grateful for the graces of this devotion, and to be most anxious that others should come to know about this extraordinary gift. Human nature never ceases to amaze me. I have known young mothers dying of cancer in a hospital bed. How I longed for the ability to visit them, and offer them a cure for their cancer that would ensure they could return to their families for many years to come. I never met anyone who would have to think twice about accepting this gift. What I am offering in this chapter is so much more important, and so much more powerful than a cure for cancer. I think of you, gentle reader, as you read these words. I hope you are well but, if you are not, I don't know what's wrong with you, or what might heal you. However, whoever you are, I am sure and certain that you need what is spoken about in this chapter. I pray that you accept the offer, and that you live to appreciate it, and that you die to really rejoice in it.

How important is forgiveness for a Christian?

'To err is human, to forgive is divine.' Forgiveness is not something that comes easily to any of us. Our feelings have been hurt, but those feelings will heal in time. However, our pride has also been hurt, and it's not so easy for that to recover. It is relatively easy for a humble person to be able to forgive. There is a need to prove ourselves right, to gain the victory in the clash of personalities, and to have the other submit to our judgement. What I am saying is a very general comment, that does not include those people who have been seriously and grievously offended, hurt, and traumatised by the brutality or perversity of another. Such people carry deep scars, and I will deal with their problem with forgiveness later on in this answer.

Most of the unforgiveness that plagues our spirit concerns relatively minor incidents. To forgive another is to set that person free, but it also includes setting myself free from the prison of resentment. Resentment is a luxury that most of us cannot afford. When I have a resentment against you, it is as if I were drinking poison, and expecting you to die! Unforgiveness is a cancer of the spirit and, like a cancer, it continues to grow and to destroy. On the other hand, forgiveness is a very real expression of love. When a couple kneel in front of me to get married, they may not have enough money or enough sense! However, if they have enough forgiveness in their hearts, I can continue the ceremony in confidence, because if they have enough forgiveness, their love will survive. When we forgive, we are following the example of God.

Yes, forgiveness is divine, and it is in God that all forgiveness is rooted. The story of redemption is the story of God's loving forgiveness. The gospel has the story of the Prodigal Son returning to the forgiving hug of the father. St John tells us that we should love one another because God has first loved us. It is the same with forgiveness. God forgives us so that we will be willing to forgive one another. Jesus taught us one simple prayer, and it is very significant that it includes the following words: 'And forgive us our trespasses as we forgive those who trespass against us.' We are compelled to set the conditions of our own forgiveness. In another place, Jesus said, 'Forgive, and you shall be forgiven.' Nothing could be simpler, and in answer to the question of how important is forgiveness in the life of the Christian, it is essential.

Jesus goes to great lengths to emphasise the importance of forgiveness. The story of the Prodigal Son is a classic. The purpose of Jesus telling a story was to ensure that his listeners grasped the core of his message. He spoke of things and situations with which they would be familiar, and to which they could relate. He told them about a servant who owed quite a lot of money to his master, and he was unable to repay him. He went to his master, and explained his predicament, and he pleaded for further time in which to repay the debt. His master went one further, and forgive him the whole debt, without any conditions attached. On his way out of the master's house, this servant met another servant who owed him a fairly paltry sum of money. He grabbed him by the throat, and began to throttle him, as he demanded the payment of the debt. The other servant pleaded with him, and begged for more time in which to repay the debt, but he was refused. He then had him thrown into jail, to remain there until the debt was paid. When the master heard what had happened, he sent for the servant and asked him, 'Is it true that, after me forgiving you your debt, you refused to forgive another servant a much smaller debt?' When this was confirmed as true, the master ordered that the servant be thrown into jail, himself and all his family, until he had completely repaid what was owed. That story speaks for itself. (May I remind you, gentle reader, of the words of Jesus, 'I never say anything unless the Father tells me to.')

On another occasion Jesus condenses this story into a question. One man was forgiven a huge debt, and another a much smaller one. Which of them would love the forgiver the most?

Which of them would be most grateful? The deeper my awareness is of my human weakness and failures, the deeper my gratitude is to the God of forgiveness.

I grew up in a time when Confession was the only sure way
of obtaining forgiveness for sin. We went to Confession every
Saturday, so we would be 'worthy' (!) enough to receive Holy
Communion on Sunday. It never occurred to me that this kind
of thinking put everybody but Roman Catholics outside the
remit of God's forgiveness! Most of the people in the world
knew nothing about Confession, and I have no memory of being
unduly concerned about that fact!

I return to Jesus' words 'Forgive, and you shall be forgiven'.
Putting it bluntly, if I want forgiveness for sin, I don't need to go
to Confession. Lest this comes across as being dismissive of the
importance of Confession, let me hasten to explain. A sacrament
is a decision that includes the grace to carry out that decision.
For example, with the sacrament of Matrimony goes the grace to
love each other 'until death do us part'. The couple may not fully
avail of this grace, and their decision may wither on the branch,
because there is nothing automatic about it. The same applies to
Ordination, which includes the grace to live the priestly life. It is
obvious that both of these sacraments have to do with the future.
In other words, they begin after those involved go outside the
door. It is the same with the sacrament of Confession. It involves
a decision about some area in my life that I decide to change, and
it includes the grace I require to put that decision into effect. For
years I was going to Confession trying to change yesterday!
Now I go to Confession with a decision that will change tomorrow.

If I wrote out all my sins, translated them into ten languages,
went to the Pope for Confession in twelve languages, and have
unforgiveness in my heart towards another human being, not
one of my sins is forgiven. There is no escape route when it
comes to forgiveness. God has entrusted me with the conditions
for my own forgiveness. In an earlier book of mine, entitled *Look
At It This Way*, the first three chapters could be summarised as

follows. In chapter one, Jesus runs after us as we leave the Garden, taps us on the shoulder and tells us that the Father wants us to return to the Garden, where a big welcoming hug awaits us (even if we have got pig's food all over our faces!). In chapter two Jesus tells us not to worry about getting back to the Garden, because he would lead us back and there was no other way of getting back. In chapter three he tells us that if we are coming back to an eternal hug, we have to become huggers on the way, when we forgive and forgive until there is no one left to forgive.

At the very beginning of this answer I said, 'To err is human, to forgive is divine.' I need to deal with this in greater detail. To be able to forgive is a gift of God's Spirit. Some years ago, a young woman died in her father's arms, after a bomb went off at a public ceremony in Northern Ireland. The father publicly and wholeheartedly forgave the perpetrators of this crime. His ability and willingness to forgive touched the whole nation, and it got worldwide publicity. As a Northern Protestant, with no political experience, he was offered, and accepted, a seat in the Senate of the Irish Republic. At that time the whole nation desperately needed the Christian witness of such a man. It is quite significant that his forgiveness should have such an effect on everyone. He was obviously a man of God, and what he did was seen as something absolutely impossible to a human being on his own.

'Father, forgive them because they know not what they do' is a powerful witness to Christian forgiveness. The apostles obviously wrestled with this idea of forgiveness, because it was so completely new to those who had been brought up to demand 'an eye for an eye, and a tooth for a tooth'. Peter asked Jesus how often he should forgive his brother if he offended him ... 'seven times?' Peter was being generous in suggesting that he should forgive all that many times! Imagine his amazement when Jesus replied 'No, not seven times, but seventy times seven!' 'Seventy times seven' was a way of saying 'no end of times'. That surely throws back the boundaries, and throws down a challenge.

Once again, I must remember that, what we are asked to do

is beyond the capacity of any human being, and is completely a grace of the Spirit. 'Lord, please give me a forgiving heart' is a prayer that we could well repeat.

Now let us deal with those who have been severely injured, or sinned against, and who cannot ever see a time coming when they will be ready, able, or willing to forgive. Straightaway, let me distinguish between forgiving and forgetting. I am speaking about the possibility of forgiving, and the probability of never being able to forget. We don't have any switches in our brains, and we cannot control our memory. However, it is possible, through the grace of God, to remove the pain and hurt from the memories, and that is done by forgiveness. This is a process, and, as such, will take its own time.

The first step is to want to forgive. I am not talking about or thinking about forgiving. All I am asking for is that I would be willing to forgive, if I were able to do so. If I have the will, the Lord will supply the power. This first step can involve a prayer for the person whom I need to forgive. At first, this prayer may be difficult, and may not come from the heart. I could find myself saying a prayer for someone, and wishing that the same person might be knocked down by a bus! That's ok. Keep the prayer going, whether a specific prayer, or a remembrance at Mass. Quite soon I will find that I am actually praying that prayer. The Spirit will be at work in the heart, and the process will have begun. Take whatever time it takes, but you can be sure of one thing: the resentment will begin to melt, and fade away. 'Peace on earth to those of goodwill'. As I said just now, if I have the will, God will give me the power to do anything. It will be interesting to experience this process unfolding, because it will be accompanied by a growth in peace, and a great sense of relief.

Strange as it may seem, the one person most of us find most difficult to forgive is ourselves. This unforgiveness is experienced as guilt. Guilt is not from God. 'I did not come to condemn the world, but to save it,' says Jesus. 'Neither do I condemn you.' In the Book of Revelations, chapter twelve, Satan is called 'The accuser of our brothers. He accuses them day and night before our God'. Guilt can be a heavy burden to carry, and Jesus invites all who are heavily-burdened to come to him, and find rest for their souls. I couldn't imagine the woman Jesus rescued from being stoned to death, or the woman who washed his feet with her tears, going down the road and living a life that was riddled with guilt. I believe that Jesus' forgiveness is total and unconditional. Jesus does not just cut the head off thistles, and leave the roots there, to grow again at a later time. When the blind man has healed, I believe that whatever caused his blindness was also healed. 'Behold I make all things new.'

If I am in tune with the Spirit, it is possible to 'feel' forgiven when I ask for forgiveness. My spirit knows when it is in tune with God, just as I am deeply aware of any alienation. Guilt is just another way of not accepting the kind of love that God offers. I can regret many things, and have remorse over others, and that's ok, except that it won't change anything. 'Lord, give me the serenity to accept the things I cannot change ...' My friend may forgive me, and I know that she forgives me, but I can very correctly continue to have remorse and regret over my actions.

Guilt, on the other hand, is a lack of belief in the sincerity or reality of the forgiveness. That could be as offensive to God as my original action. Forgiveness is a very real, and a very powerful form of love, and God is into forgiveness in a very big way. He leaves all judgement till judgement day, and he asks us to do the same. We are asked to forgive, not to judge, and not to condemn, and he promises that he will treat us in exactly the same way. 'Do to others as you would like them to do to you.'

The question posed was, 'How important is forgiveness for a Christian?' I hope, in trying to reply, that I have shown that it is central, essential, and at the very heart of Christian living. Whenever I pray with someone for healing, I expect something to happen. Either the person gets better, or experiences a real peace and acceptance. If nothing happens, then I know there is a barrier somewhere within that person's soul. I'm sure there can be many barriers to the action of the Spirit, but the one I generally find is unforgiveness. I sit with those people, and go back down the road of life with them, in an attempt to uncover that unforgiveness. In most cases we unearth it, and the Spirit is free to act. Unforgiveness is such a serious barrier that it can block the way to eternal salvation. Nobody could be happy while unforgiveness gnaws away in their heart. Forgiveness involves throwing the prison door open, and being free again. The connection between forgiveness, happiness, and the presence of the Spirit is all-binding. They go together, and they form the constituents of a happy life. God wants to forgive us; he wants us to forgive others; and he wants us to forgive ourselves. All of this is yet another expression of his great love for us. 'Father, forgive them ...' were among the final words of Jesus.

How should a Christian face up to death?

I wrote a booklet about thirty years ago entitled *Good News About Death*. In the introduction I said that I became interested in this subject, because I was puzzled by the fact that a Christian could be afraid of dying. If I really accept the whole of the gospel message, I must accept that it deals with dying as well as living. Death, with sin and sickness, was one of the three weeds that Satan ('the evil one') sowed in the field of good wheat. When the servants offered to remove the weeds, the master said 'No, No! Leave them there, and I myself will remove them because, in pulling up the weeds, you are likely to damage the wheat as well.' Jesus came to remove these three weeds because, of ourselves, we could do nothing about them. Death was the 'final enemy', and everything hinged on Jesus overcoming death and showing that he had the victory. 'If Jesus had not risen from the dead, our faith is in vain,' St Paul tells us. It was very important for Jesus to impress on his apostles that he had actually risen from the dead, that he was alive, and the victory was his. He spent forty days with them to reinforce this belief, and would have spent more if that were needed. In the Mass, when we speak about Jesus, we speak in the past tense: 'Dying you *destroyed* our death, rising you *restored* our life …' 'Lord, by your cross and resurrection, *you have set us free* …'

Let me try to put death in context. Once life begins, it never ends. The first stage is the womb life. Then comes a breaking, a wrenching, as the baby emerges into the womb of life. That ends with yet another breaking or wrenching, as that person passes on to the fullness of life. It is then, and not till then, that the person becomes all that God created her to be. The person is now complete, and has reached the fullness of life. When a baby is born the only thing we can be certain of is that this baby will die one day. If I draw a line on a wall, and continue on towards the horizon, putting two marks a few inches apart on that line, this would help illustrate that I spend an infinitesimal amount of my exisence in the body. The body is not me. I am just living in the body for a certain length of time. The photo on the cover of this book is of a 73-year old man! The *body* is 73 years old, but the real me, the person *inside the body*, is still a child, never grows old, and continues to need being loved, and being liked.

John Quincey Adams was President of the United States one time. He was a ponderous philosophical man, who wouldn't use six words when twenty would do! As a frail old man, he met someone as he walked along, leaning on his canc. 'How is Mr John Quincey Adams today?' he was asked. 'Mr John Quincey Adams is well, thank you', came the reply. 'The dwelling in which he lives is becoming very unreliable. The foundations are no longer too secure, the roof is beginning to come apart, and the walls are no longer very sturdy. Soon this dwelling will become uninhabitable, and Mr John Quincey Adams will have to change residence, and go to live elsewhere. But, in answer to your question, kind sir, today Mr John Quincey Adams is well, thank you.'

I will never go into a coffin. The body in which I spent my life here on earth will be no longer needed, and it can be buried, cremated, or donated for medical research. When the American space shuttle has been launched, the booster rockets, which gave it propulsion and direction, can be discarded and fall back to earth. They have done their job and are no longer needed. It is the same with the body. The body will become so dysfunctional as to be no longer viable and I will have to vacate it and go to live elsewhere.

For some years past, people like Kübler Ross, Moody, etc., have explored what is called 'near-death' experiences. People who were actually dying, were revived with an electric shock or by some other means. Many of them had begun to experience what they described as travelling towards a tunnel of light, into a sense of extraordinary peace. Some of them got so far along the journey that they saw those who had gone before them coming to meet them. Many of them were bitterly disappointed when they revived, and they felt cheated. For them, all fear of death was gone forever. I myself interviewed a Dominican priest who had 'died' in Trinidad many years before that. His experiences were quite convincing, and really consoling. He has since passed on, but I could easily imagine that that final call was something which held no fear for him.

There is quite a wide chasm between the three stages of life. If the unborn could hear you, there is not one word that the baby would understand. Water? Light? House? No, you're wasting your time. It is the same with those who have gone ahead of us. 'No one comes back to tell us', we may say. The real truth is that they would be wasting their time, because 'eye has not seen, nor ear heard, nor has it entered into the heart of man/woman to imagine what God has in store for those who love him'. Our deceased relatives have not gone away, they have simply gone ahead. They are waiting for us and, effectively, they will be our midwives when our time comes to be born into eternal life. The parents are with their children in the park. The children run ahead, over the brow of a hill, and they crouch down as if hiding. The parents cannot see them, but they know that they will soon come into view, as they themselves reach the top of that hill. It is simply a case of '*au revoir* and not goodbye'.

Hope in the face of death is at the heart of the Christian message. Jesus is our Moses, leading us through the desert of life, through the Red Sea of death, into the Promised Land of heaven. Where he goes, we expect to follow. When he says 'Follow me', he is not speaking about just the few years of my life here on earth. Jesus tells us, 'In my Father's house there are many mansions. If it were not so, I would have told you. I am going to prepare a place for you. Then I will come and bring you so that, where I am, you also will be.'

A few years ago I wrote a book called *Jesus Said It And I Believe It*, which was based on 57 promises Jesus makes in the gospels. Many of those promises have to do with death. Jesus said, 'The sin of this world is unbelief in me', and 'When the Son of Man comes will he find any faith on this earth?' My generation thought of death as that time when I appear before God, and 'render an account of my stewardship'. This was an encounter that we dreaded, and had every reason to do so. I no longer think of death in this way. In fact, to be honest, I don't give much thought at all to life after death. I have decided that I will pack in as much living as I can before death. I am more concerned about life before death than life after death!

Everybody dies, but not everybody lives. Some people settle for existing and, when they die, we have to get a doctor to certify it, because there was never much life there in the first place! You could write on a tombstone, 'Died at forty, buried at eighty'! I myself am 'retired' (?!) for some years now but, thank God, I continue to be as busy as I have ever been. I would much prefer to burn out than to rust out! We will be dead long enough, so let us live life to the full while we have the time. 'Work away while you have daylight', says Jesus, 'because the time will come when no one can work.'

I am prepared to face death with one conviction: That Jesus has done enough to merit my redemption and salvation, and I trust in him to do that for me. That is the beginning and end of my hope. It is his blood and our faith, as we are told in the letter to the Romans. I believe that I am going to heaven when I die because Jesus died to earn that for me, and for no other reason. St Thérèse of Lisieux was quite heretical in her views, relative to the theology of her day. God created us to 'know, love and serve him, and by this means to gain everlasting life' was the teaching from her day that continued on to mine. It was against this backdrop that she spoke of going to heaven, of appearing before God with empty hands, of God's love being more than sufficient to make all things right. She could well have been accused of the sin of presumption. I thank God that I have lived long enough to see her proclaimed a Doctor of the Church, when her teaching has become official church teaching.

I know the Way to heaven, and that Way is Jesus. 'No one comes to the Father except through me', Jesus tells us. To trust Jesus enough that I really do believe that he will keep all of his promises, is a sure and certain guarantee of entry into the fullness of God's Kingdom. Elizabeth said to Mary, 'All these things happened to you, because you believed that the promises of the Lord would be fulfilled.'

St Padre Pio and St Thérèse of Lisieux, among others, give us yet another great hope in death. They said that their real work would begin after they died. This makes a great deal of sense, and it is a great consolation. I dealt with this in an earlier answer about the Communion of Saints. I myself have entrusted very special intentions to the terminally ill, asking them to attend to the problem when they came before the throne of God. I always expected that prayer to be answered, and I have never been disappointed. My parents continue to be my parents, just as Mary continues to be the Mother of Jesus. I expect my parents to be more than interested in what affects my well-being down here. We all have 'friends in high places', and the time will come when we will be able to shower many blessings on those who come behind us.

The very first question I chose for this book is one about God being love. All of Jesus' life and death was to convince us of this, and the greatest thanks I could offer for the graces that Jesus earned for me is to be humble enough to allow that love reach me, and protect me. When I asked an elderly lady, within sight of death, if she had any fear about meeting God, her answer was instant and very powerful: 'Father, I'm sure he's going to be very glad to see me.' The father of the prodigal is scanning the horizon, awaiting our return to the Garden.

I wrote earlier about Jesus overcoming death, through his own death and resurrection. It is also very significant that he could stretch out a hand and restore life to the daughter of Jairus, or the son of the widow of Naim. Jesus acted out of compassion, even though he didn't do the family any great favour, in so far as that person had to pass through the trauma of death a second time. I don't pretend to understand what is called 'the mystery of death'. Death seems to be both deaf and blind, and it seldom comes at the right time. It makes little distinction between the cot-death baby, and the centenarian who is completely out of touch with reality for many years now. There seems to be little rhyme or reason to the selection process.

In actual practice, I like to think that God has very little to do with this selection process. The functioning and condition of the body is the chief determinant in the time of death, apart, of course, from those who are killed or who choose to end their lives. St Padre Pio is a good example of a death that was obviously part of the divine plan for him. He knew beforehand when he was going to die, his tomb was prepared in advance, and he died on the fiftieth anniversary of receiving the stigmata. I don't think that many of us can claim to be part of such a divine plan. People get cancer because their body cells are susceptible to something in the environment or in their food. A twin brother could be immune from cancer, but might be a prime candidate for diabetes. I imagine that the metabolism of the body is more of a determinant of the nature and severity of our illnesses than anything to do with a divine decision. My mother died of throat cancer, even though she never smoked a cigarette in her life.

Because of the nature of the question, it is beyond my remit to deal with bereavement, dealing with terminally ill, etc. My answer has more to do with that question that puzzled me all those years ago about a Christian being afraid of dying. 'Fear not' were the most frequently used words in the teachings of Jesus. St John tells us, 'Perfect love drives out all fear. If we are afraid, it is because we fear what God might do to us, and, if we are afraid of what God might do to us, it shows us that we're not yet fully convinced that God loves us.'

Accepting and facing death as a friend is the ultimate test of our conviction about God's love. When, like Jesus, we can breathe our last and trust the Father to 'catch' us as we fall into his arms, is the acid test of our faith. And that truth is at the kernel of my answer to the question. 'The saint is not the person who loves God, but the person who is totally convinced that God loves her' is a quote that I have used in other answers, and that applies very directly here. Death is a fact of life! When the baby is born, the cord is cut, just as the straps are pulled up from the coffin after it is has been lowered into the grave. The cord is cut yet again, as the person passes on to the third and final part of life. Death is the greatest 'kick' of all, and maybe that's why it's kept till last! A worthwhile life has been defined thus: 'When you were born, you alone cried, and everybody else was very happy. Live your life in such a way that, when you die, you will be very happy, and everyone else will be crying!' Or to quote Mark Twain, 'You should live your life in such a way that, when you die, even the undertaker will be sorry!'

How can I be a Peacemaker?

'Blessed are the peacemakers, for they shall be called the children of God.' That is quite a title, and that alone should motivate me to find out what makes for a peacemaker, and how to become one.

Peace involves freedom from, or cessation of a war. Peace is what I experience when my relationships are the way they ought to be. Peace is not something that just happens; it has to be made to happen. One of the ways of understanding peace is to consider its opposite. Conflict, violence, war, aggression, and murder are things that disturb the soul. Our inner spirits cannot feel at home with these, so they must surely run counter to the instincts of our nature. The spirit withers in such an atmosphere, while it blooms and blossoms in an atmosphere of tranquillity.

Remember that Jesus is not speaking about those who *have* peace, but about those who *make* peace. To be a reconciler in the lives of others presupposes a soul that is reconciled with itself, with God, and with life. Peace can result from a resolved dispute, a truce or ceasefire, but peace is so much more than the absence of war. I have been in Belfast during some of the several 'ceasefires'. There were no bombs or bullets, but there was no peace either. There was a tension in the air, and a great lack of trust in every person and every action that occurred around me. I felt a need to keep looking over my shoulder all the time.

Jesus raises the bar when he speaks about peace. He offers us *his peace*. He tells us that this is not the peace the world gives. 'Peace be with you; I give you my peace. Not as the world gives peace do I give it to you. Do not be troubled; do not be afraid.' On a few occasions after his resurrection, he appeared to the apostles in a room, and his first action was to breathe his Spirit on them, and his first words were, 'Peace be with you.'

Peace is the result or the outcome of something. That is what I understand from what Jesus has said. It may seem strange to hear him say that he did not come to bring peace. His coming among us would cause great conflict, because we would be forced to take sides, to make up our minds, to decide either for him or against him. Jesus said that this could set brother against brother, or father against son. Simeon prophesied that Jesus would be 'a sign of contradiction'. His coming would challenge us to take him seriously and follow him. To do nothing is, in itself, a decision. We cannot escape this challenge, and we have a straight choice between conflict or peace. Jesus offers us peace, but we do not have to accept it. Good will always be opposed by evil. It will always be put to the test. When we make a decision relative to deepening our commitment to Jesus, we may well experience disquiet within at the thought of what this is going to entail, or what it's going to cost me. The well-meaning advice from family and relatives will also put our resolve to the test.

It is in breaking through, in breaking out of this conflict, that peace is to be found. Peace is like the treasure hidden in a field which, when we find it, we are ready and willing to sell all we have to purchase that field. The peacemakers are the peaceseekers. Rather than being the absence of war, peace is the presence of something. This is something that we can seek, and in seeking we will find.

There has never been a bullet fired or a bomb planted that did not begin in the heart of a human being. The action is but the outcome of a decision. The same can be said about peace, which must begin in the hearts of people before they can effect that peace in their surroundings. In the Beatitudes, Jesus speaks of the peacemakers, the meek, and the gentle almost in the same breath. These are special people, people of the Spirit. They form the leaven that affects all around them. A few good people in an area can prevent the whole place becoming corrupt and evil.

Jesus speaks about evil coming out of the hearts of people. 'From the abundance of the heart the mouth speaks.' All conflicts and wars begin there. No wonder he attributes the title 'children of God' to those who are free from such evil. All peacemaking must begin in the heart. The gospels present us with many incidents involving reconciliation. The Forgiving Father was most anxious to bring reconciliation between the Prodigal Son and his self-righteous brother. Jesus was concerned about Mary being able to accept her sister Martha 'who was busy about many things'. Jesus listened quietly to his disciples arguing about which of them was the greatest, and then he confronted them. His calming of the storm on the Sea of Galilee was a symbol of what he wished to do in the hearts of all his people. When Jesus entered the house of Zaccheus he said, 'Salvation has come to this house today.' Peace is about right relationships, and I am challenged, when in the presence of Jesus, to ensure that my relationships are the way they ought to be. When the Samaritan woman at the well waffled on about where we should worship, Jesus simply asked her to go and get her husband! That stopped her in her tracks, because she was presently the wife of husband number seven!

When Jesus sent his disciples out to preach, he gave them some important last-minute instructions. 'Whatever house you enter, first bless them, saying "Peace to this house." If a peaceful person lives there, the peace shall rest upon him. But, if not, the blessing will return to you.' Jesus is very definite in his instructions about dealing with those who do not accept that offer of peace. 'But in any town where you are not welcomed, go to the marketplace and proclaim: "Even the dust of your town that clings to our feet, we wipe off, and leave with you. Yet know and be sure that the kingdom of God has come to you".'

Senator George Mitchell of the US is a name that deserves to be enshrined with honour in the history of Northern Ireland. He came there as a peacemaker when few people could have hoped for peace. He took the flak from both sides and, even he, at times, must have despaired of ever bringing those opposing factions together. His greatest weapon was his own imperturbability, and his ability to remain neutral. The man of peace has a power that the world cannot deal with. Mahatma Ghandi and Martin Luther King were assassinated because that was the only way their opponents could think of silencing them. Thankfully,

George Mitchell was not assassinated, and finally the opposing factions came around to listening to him. His greatest power was his gentleness, and this was obvious as one listened to him speak.

Tony Blair has retired as leader of the Labour Party, and as Prime Minister of England, and at present his legacy is being reviewed. No matter how negative some of those reviews might be, no one can take from him the credit he deserves for completing the work of reconciliation in Northern Ireland. Both himself and the Irish Taoiseach (Prime Minister) needed endless patience and tolerance, to be able to sustain the momentum of the process, and see it to completion. If they themselves were not reasonably mature and well-balanced individuals, they would have generated even further antagonism, and we would still be living with the horror. Yes, indeed, 'blessed are the peacemakers'.

God is Love is a phrase that is getting more frequent mention these days, due in no small part to the first letter of Pope Benedict XVI. It is logical to presume from this that 'children of God' must imply those who share in that love. 'By this shall all people know that you are my disciples if you have love one for another.' Those with love in their hearts bring peace with them wherever they go, just as those with anger, turmoil, or aggression spread those seeds along the path of their lives. The peacemakers are real treasures wherever they go.

Peace is one of the fruits of the Spirit, or one of those blessings that come from using the gifts of the Spirit. If the Spirit is not its origin then it is simply like 'the peace that the world gives'. No UN or NATO forces can bring peace. They may stop a war, but it will break out down the road in a short period of time. There can be no lasting peace in the world without God's Spirit. Therefore, it is reasonable to say and realistic to accept that there will never be lasting peace on this earth.

Every summer we witness a recurring problem, either in California, Australia, or such hot spots. They have forest fires that ravage large areas, and cost millions of dollars. The emergency services attack the fire with every resource they have. It must be very frustrating to have extinguished the fire in a large area, only to see it break out again in an area that they thought was safe. They never know where the next flames may begin.

The forces that enter an area to bring peace, are contributing a very real service to humanity, even if, at the best of times, they are nothing better than a fire brigade. At the moment we are witnessing what is happening in Iraq, as a result of that country being invaded in an effort to restore democracy there! They can send in as many soldiers as they have, but they cannot 'impose' peace on the country. Peace must begin in the hearts of the people, and not out of the muzzle of the gun of the invader. It is at this stage that we could hope and pray for another George Mitchell, who would pave the way for reconciliation, rather than increase the forces, and the determination to crush all opposition.

Nobody wins a war. The very fact that I go to war in the first place is an admission of failure on my part. I lived in the US during the Vietnam war, and nothing much has changed since then. A short while ago, the US President visited Vietnam and received a civic reception there, while those accompanying him made several trade agreements. It is sad that so many had to die before we could arrive at this stage. It is sadder still to think of the many innocent ones who got caught up in the hellfire of war, and who paid with their lives for the stubbornness and stupidity of others. The First World War was a war that was fought 'to end all wars'. The countries involved had just recovered when the armies were on the war-path again, and countless millions were eliminated in the cauldron of fire that followed. This war saw the horrors of Hiroshima and Nagasaki, as well as the nightmare horrors of the concentration camps. And even that war did not 'end all wars'. 'Man's inhumanity to man makes countless thousands mourn' wrote Bobby Burns.

The more aware I am of the various conflicts that bedevil our world, the more obvious it must be of the need for peacemakers. On my own I can feel helpless to affect the wider situation.

'What are these among so many?' the apostles asked, as they looked at their few loaves and the thousands who were hungry. This feeling of inadequacy should not be an excuse for inaction. We all can do something. It is said that the hardest place to prac- tise the gospel is in our own kitchens. At Cana, they only had water, and for the hungry thousands they had a few loaves and fish. However, when those were made available to Jesus, there was more than enough and, indeed, there was plenty left over. 'Whatever you have is enough' is a good reminder to all of us. Do you think that Blessed Mother Teresa hoped to be able to feed all the hungry people in India? I don't think so, but that didn't stop her from trying. If I am not part of the solution, I con- tinue to be part of the problem.

Being at peace with myself, and being at peace with the world is a beautiful feeling that makes such a difference in life. If I cannot live with myself, I will not do too well in living with others. When Jesus arrived in this world, the heavens pro- claimed, 'Peace on earth to those of goodwill.'

In this answer we are dealing with being a peacemaker but, of course, if I do not *have* peace, I cannot be a peacemaker. 'Lord, give me the serenity to accept the things I cannot change, courage to change the things I can, and the wisdom to know the difference.' If you want to change the world you have to begin with yourself because, in the final analysis, that is the only part of the world over which you can have control. I pray for the courage to change the things I can. Ensuring peace in my own heart and home is my biggest contribution to peace in the world. 'If each before his own door swept, the whole village would be clean' is a wise old Chinese proverb.

Part of this process of reconciliation involves making friends with my shadow. Like the moon, I tend to keep the bright side out for people to see. But there is a dark side that I may not ac- cept, and it can cause quite a lot of guilt, and a constant sense of failure. The next question I will deal with has to do with uncon- ditional love. An important part of the answer will have to do with love of self, which is a very healthy thing, as opposed to self-love, which is pride. If guilt and condemnation do not come from God, which they don't, then they must come from Satan, or from my own wounded pride. Imagine what would happen if I became a peacemaker to myself! I am not speaking about having a 'fool's pardon' for wrong-doing, giving me a *carte blanche* to do as I please. I am speaking about wrong-doing that is repented, has received God's forgiveness, and is still in need of my own forgiveness. If I have to become perfect before I can become a peacemaker, the world should not hold its breath! We are not saints. All we can do is do the best with what we have. My own inner peace grows with every effort I make to establish peace among others.

The whole process is an end in itself. It is a cyclic process, in that establishing peace in my own heart, and among the people with whom I live, go side by side. This is a win-win situation, and to hear the call to become involved is certainly the voice of God's Spirit. Learning to live and to walk in the Spirit is a sure and certain way of 'guiding my feet into the way of peace'.

The question being dealt with is about how I could become a peacemaker. I didn't go into any great detail about how best I could do that. Let me finish by saying that if the Spirit of God is in every word I speak, and in everything I do, then I am a peacemaker right there. I can sit down in a kitchen where the pots and pans are flying, take a deep breath, and gently speak from the heart. Through the Spirit I ensure that I am immune to the tensions and angers all around me. I speak words of peace and, even in the silences, my heart is whispering a prayer for peace.

The presence of God's Spirit is like pouring oil on troubled waters. Jesus asked us to do what he did. He calmed the storm, and brought a calm, and there are situations in which we are asked to do the same. Through his Spirit, Jesus is continuing his work through us. At best we are but channels. 'Make me a channel of your peace. Where there is hatred, let me bring your love. Where there is injury, your pardon, Lord.' We are channels, not generators or transformers. The Spirit of God can use any one of us as a peacemaker.

What is meant by 'Unconditional Love'?

I will begin with a story. A retired missionary in Ireland tells the following story. He was working in the bush in Africa. Once a month the 'flying doctors' came by in a helicopter, and spent a day treating patients that had gathered for them. On one occasion one of the patients was a young lad who had a very nasty harelip. He arrived at the mission station with his parents, and most of his extended family. One of the doctors did plastic surgery, and it was hoped that he would do something for this young lad. The young lad entered the tent on Friday evening, and spent the rest of that day, and all that night there. He emerged from the tent before noon on the following day. The surgeon had done a wonderful job, which could be plainly seen through the transparent dressing that covered his upper lip. His father was seated under a tree opposite the makeshift clinic. The young lad approached him, bowed his head for the father's blessing, and then walked away towards the other members of his family. There was no reaction, or not a word from the father. When the rest of the family saw his lip they were really excited. They danced with joy, and hugged him with delight. The priest was watching the father, and there was still no response from him. This annoyed the priest, who approached the old man and asked 'Did you see the job the doctor did on your son's lip?' 'Yes, I did', came the reply. 'Were you pleased with the job that was done on him?' 'Oh, yes, I was very pleased indeed', said the old man. With a bite in his voice the priest said, 'Well, you didn't show any great excitement when your son came to show you the results of the doctor's work!' 'I love my son', replied the old man, 'and I have always loved my son. If I showed any great excitement now, that would show him that I hadn't really loved him when he had a harelip.' That is unconditional love!

The first question in this book is about God being love. In other words, 'God' and 'love' are words that are interchangeable. God is *love*, not just some dimension of love. I can love music, my sister, or visiting the local Chinese restaurant. There are endless dimensions of love, each of which is but a tiny part of the whole. I can hear music that I don't like; my sister can annoy me at times; and there are times when I promise myself a break from Chinese food! Unconditional love is pure love, with no price tags, and no strings attached.

When St Paul speaks about love, he places no limits on its scope, or its centrality. 'Love is patient, kind, without envy. It is not boastful or arrogant. It is not ill-mannered, nor does it seek its own interest. Love overcomes anger and forgets offences. It does not take delight in wrong, but rejoices in truth. Love excuses everything, believes all things, hopes all things, endures all things. Love will never end.' This kind of love, of course, is not human love, which is as limited as we are.

This love is pure gift, and it is one of the most precious gifts of the Spirit. This is not something I can practise and become good at, like jogging in preparation for a marathon. Again and again and again I have to throw the door of my heart wide open, and ask the Spirit, 'Please fill me with your love.'

Unconditional love means loving others as God loves us. By ourselves, on our own, this is not possible for a human. Every human is mortal and will die, and everything that is human, like human love, will also die. On my own, I am like a tape-recorder with batteries. I can play, of course, but don't expect me to continue playing after the batteries have run low. Unconditional love is the tape-recorder that is plugged into a socket and is drawing from a power that is not its own.

May I continue with another story? Two men, both seriously ill, occupied the same hospital room. One man was allowed sit up in his bed for an hour each afternoon to help drain the fluid from his lungs. His bed was next to the room's only window. The other man had to spend all his time lying flat on his back, because of an injured spine. The men talked for hours on end. They spoke of their wives and families, their homes, their jobs, their involvement in the military service, and where they had been on vacation. Every afternoon, when the man in the bed by the window could sit up, he would pass the whole time describing to his room-mate all the things he could see outside the window. The man in the other bed began to live for those one-hour periods, when the world would be broadened and enlivened by all the activity and colour of the world outside. The window overlooked a park with a lovely lake. Ducks and swans moved along in the water, while children sailed their model boats. Young lovers walked arm in arm amidst flowers of every colour, and a fine view of the city skyline could be seen in the distance. As the man by the window described all this in exquisite detail, the man on the other side of the room would close his eyes, and imagine the picturesque scene. One warm afternoon the man by the window described a parade passing by. Although the other couldn't hear the band, he could see it in his mind's eye, as the man by the window portrayed it with descriptive words. Days and weeks passed. One morning the day nurse arrived to bring water for their baths, only to find the lifeless body of the man by the window, who had died during the night. She was saddened, and called the hospital attendants to take the body away. As soon as it seemed appropriate, the other man asked if he could be moved next to the window. The nurse was happy to make the switch and, making sure he was comfortable, she left him alone. Slowly, painfully, he propped himself up on one elbow to take his first look at the real world outside. He strained to slowly turn to look out the window by his bed. It faced a blank wall! The man asked the nurse what could have compelled the other man to describe such wonderful things outside his window, when there was nothing there but a blank wall. The nurse replied that the man was blind, and could not even see the wall. She said, 'He was the kindest man I have ever met, and I will never forget him. Everything he did for you was just his way of helping you, and making life easier for you.' That was unconditional love.

Such love has no price tags attached. For many years, Blessed Mother Teresa gave witness to the world of a love that was unconditional. Her love was not determined by the appreciation and thanks of others, and for those who were so mentally disabled as to be incapable of showing appreciation, her love was all the greater. She was loving them as she knew that God loved her. That is the kind of love that Jesus asked for. 'You must love one another as I have loved you', Jesus told us. This love can only be given by those who have the Spirit of God within them.

The charism of my own Congregation, the Sacred Hearts of Jesus and Mary, speaks of providing a human face for the love of God, as we minister to others. We are asked to provide the hands, the voice, the ears, and expect God to provide the love. Blessed Damien, a member of my Congregation, who lived and died with the lepers on the island of Molokai, was another very authentic witness to this kind of love. Because of their human condition, and the colony of death to which society had condemned them, he dared not speak to them about God's love, because they had every reason to be angry and to blame God for the situation in which they found themselves. However, over time, and a constant dying to himself, he himself came to love them. They came to believe that he loved them, and it was only then that he dared speak of God's love. In himself, he incarnated that love to them, and gave them a reason for living, and a purpose for dying. It was his love, and his love alone, that transformed their lives, and motivated them to care for and to love each other.

God's love was made incarnate in Jesus Christ. He hugged the children, accepted the sinner, and touched the leper. He gave witness to an extraordinary love, and the most marginalised and the greatest outcasts felt safe in his presence. He was disappointed when only one of the ten lepers returned to give thanks for being healed. He did not regret healing them, and the ungrateful ones remained healed, but he was disappointed for them because they were most to be pitied if unable to be grateful. To be grateful is to be happy, and he was sad that they set limits to his healing, which did not go any deeper than their leprous skins. When Jesus provides, he provides in abundance. 'I came that you should have life, and have it in abundance.' When he turned the water into wine at Cana, the young couple had more wine that they could possibly need. When he multiplied the loaves and fish, there were baskets of food left over. Ours is a generous God, and generosity is seen at its best in unconditional love.

Jesus made no distinction whatever between Jew or Samaritan, between religious leader or public sinner. God has no grandchildren; we are all children of God. His greatest problem was with the religious leaders, because they were hidebound by rules, conditions, and stipulations of conduct, to such an extent that many groups of people were seen as being outside the pale of their love. They must have been shocked to hear Jesus telling them that they should love their enemies! They believed in retribution, 'an eye for an eye, and a tooth for a tooth'. They must have been really puzzled (and annoyed) by Jesus when he said, 'If you love only those who love you, what thanks do you deserve? Even the pagans do that, do they not? And if you give to those who give to you, surely the heathens do as much, don't they?' He demanded a very high standard of love; nothing less than his own love for us.

He knew well, of course, that what he was asking was too much for us, but he also knew what would happen when the Spirit came. He longed for that day, because, only then could his kingdom be established on this earth. The kingdom of God is built by tiny acts, and most of them are hidden. Everyone of us has many many opportunities every day to say the kind word, to do the kind deed. Most people will not be aware of our motives, and the good words and deeds are better because of that. I know a lady who said a Rosary every single day for twenty five years for her alcoholic brother. He has found sobriety, and he has no idea that his sister played a big part in that. She didn't do it for his gratitude, but for his good. That is unconditional love.

'They who live in love, live in God, and God lives in them.' This is the most wonderful and exciting part of unconditional love. It is what happens when God makes his home in us. 'Many sins are forgiven her because she has loved much' was the verdict of Jesus on the public sinner who washed his feet with her tears. What Jesus was saying is that she could not possibly be alienated from God, and love the way she does. If she has such love, then she must surely have God. That was quite a challenge to the religious leaders who were convinced in their outright condemnation of the woman, and indeed of Jesus, for having anything to do with her. Once again, we encounter the age-old problem between the love of law and the law of love.

Love of law can be very destructive, and when promotion of a law is put above the welfare of the person, many innocent people are made to suffer. When Jesus looked at people, he saw the reality, he saw the person. He didn't label them 'Samaritans', 'lepers', 'prostitutes', or 'tax collectors'. Each was a person, and he treated them as such. Each of them had feelings, had needs, and they liked to be liked, and they loved to be loved. Not much difference between them and any of the rest of us.

One of the best examples of unconditional love is the story of the Prodigal Son. The father's love was unconditional and his forgiveness was total. When the son returned, the father set no conditions on his welcome. He even gave him sandals, which was a way of saying that the son was free to leave again if he so wished. I remember coming out of a Dublin hospital late one night, where I had been at the death-bed of a parishioner. As I came down the front steps, there was a man there, wrapped in an old coat against the freezing elements. He asked me for some money and a cigarette. I was in one of my more generous moods, so I sat beside him on the step, gave him some money, and I offered to join him in a smoke. I was shocked when I sat next to him, because he was so much younger than I had at first imagined. In answer to my questions, he told me where he was from, how and why his life had taken a turn-down, and how he ended up sleeping rough on the city streets. After a few more cigarettes, I got up to leave. Imagine my embarrassment and surprise when the young man held out his hand, with my money in it, and offered to return it to me! To him, I had given him more than money by spending some time with him, and the money was no longer important. Needless to say I would not accept the money, and I went on my way. However, I have often thought of that young man, and I am still grateful for what he gave me. That was unconditional love.

It doesn't come naturally to us to love unconditionally. Under ideal circumstances, a newborn baby receives unconditional love. What helps at this stage is that the parents are in control; they are calling the shots. However, when that child comes to its second birth, moving from the dependent stage to the independent stage, it is natural to begin to expect some return for all the love they have lavished. At the age of twelve, however, the youth is essentially self-preoccupied, being concerned about peer groups, how others perceive him/her, and interests that differ quite a lot from those of the parents. Tension begins to enter the relationship at this stage, and it can become almost impossible for the parents to continue loving unconditionally. This can be a 'rocky' part of their journey together, and, for a while, the parents may experience that they have a 'stranger' in the house. All will be well, though, if the parents come to realise that they need even more love now than they had for the newly-born! Love will always triumph, and it is a road without landmines. While the parents may be concerned about what they should be doing to help their child through these 'tender years', they may well forget how much they have to gain in the process. If their love continues to be there, through thick and thin, both child and parents are greatly blessed. No matter what they buy their children for birthdays or Christmas, the greatest gift they can give is unconditional love. Naturally, unconditional love does not mean allowing the child a free hand to do as he/she pleases. God forbid! Of course, it will involve setting boundaries, and giving guidance, but all of this will be done in love. The spirit in my voice, the tone of voice I use, will be the determinant factor in whether I am 'driving' the child, or walking alongside her. 'Don't walk in front, I may not follow. Don't walk behind, I may not lead. Just walk beside me, and be my friend.'

The question posed was 'What is meant by Unconditional

Love?' The answer, I hope, is nothing less than us passing on to others the kind of love we receive from God. This is an extraordinary call, and a source of great and many blessings for us all. We should pray for this gift, we should long for it. The world and its people desperately need this love. 'Where there is no love, sow love, and there you will find love' are words attributed to St Ireneus.

The parable of the sower in the gospels is highly significant. The sower scattered the seed in all directions. That is what he went out to do. He was not responsible for what happened to the seed after that. Some of it failed to give any return, and some of it gave different levels of return; some even returning 100%. Let us sow the seed of love, and allow people the freedom to accept it, or neglect it. When we die, we will not be asked what the other person did with the love we offered. What matters is that we will have given it away. That is unconditional love.

How is it possible to 'Be not afraid'?

'Fear not; be not afraid' are probably the most used words in all of the gospels. It is interesting to note that it is always used at a time of divine intervention, as if the normal response of the human to the divine were one of fear. I will speak about this later on in the answer.

When the Archangel appeared to Mary, his first words were 'Fear not'. It was the same when the angels appeared to the shepherds. Even Jesus had to use these words on some of the occasions when he appeared to his disciples after his resurrection. It seems that anything that brings us outside the circle of our normal everyday experiences is a cause of fear for us. We are afraid of the unknown.

This has often been evident to me regarding animals. Most times, the dog that bites is the one that is afraid. Once I befriend him, and he gets to know and trust me, he will never even bark at me again. When he has no reason to trust me, he will be ready to protect himself. When he discovers that he has generated fear in me, he enjoys the victory and can become a bully. The proper approach is to stand up to him and, at the same time, to give him reason to trust you.

The Archangel and the angels had a message, and they needed to eliminate fear before their message could be delivered and received. 'Fear' is defined as 'an unpleasant emotion caused by exposure to danger; expectation of pain, etc.' Fear is a natural emotion when we are exposed to something we do not trust. I inherited a real fear of thunder and lightning from my mother. At the first sound of thunder the curtains were drawn, the candles were lit, the holy water was sprinkled, and the Rosary beads were handed out to each of us. It took me years to get rid of this fear! I cannot remember availing of any divine intervention in freeing myself. The only thing I can put it down to is finding myself standing, as a teacher, in front of a class of young

131

children, in the middle of a thunderstorm! I had no choice but to be brave! I didn't hear anyone saying, 'Fear not; be not afraid', but I knew that I was saying this to myself! One or two such experiences helped free me from this fear.

Some years ago I developed a great fear of flying. I don't know where this came from because I had very few bad experiences. It lasted for several years and, as my life involved flying back and forth to the US at the time, it caused me great anxiety, and the fear was sometimes paralysing. I have a friend who went to an airport on three separate mornings, and he had to come away because of the terror he experienced at the thought of boarding a plane. In my own case, my fear seems to have gone just as simply as it came. I cannot explain or understand either, but I would have to accept that divine intervention was very much part of freedom from this particular fear.

The fear that I want to deal with first is the fear that has to do with things of God. Going back to the second question in this book about what the gospels tell us about God, I would remind you, gentle reader, that when you think of God, always think of Jesus. I wrote, in my answer to that question, how my generation had a God of fear, a God who watched us all the time, a God we couldn't trust, and a God who was going to have the final say in our eternal destination. I could not trust that God, and, therefore, I was afraid of him. The Father sent Jesus down among us, and if anything was to come out of that, surely it should be to eliminate any fear we might still have. The children had no reason to be afraid of Jesus. The prostitute had every reason, but somehow as with the public sinner who walked straight into where Jesus was in the house of the Pharisee, she had no fear whatever in his presence. As a matter of fact, Jesus was the only person in that house that she was not afraid of.

'Perfect love drives out all fear. We need have no fear of those who love us perfectly. If we are afraid, it is for fear of what he might do to us. And, if we are afraid of what he might do to us, this shows that we do not believe that God really loves us.' The children were not afraid of Jesus, as they climbed on his knee, and he hugged them. Children are very quick to pick up whether a person or a situation is 'safe' or not. They will go straight to some people, and shy away from others.

The more I consider the gospel scenes the more inclined I am to come to Jesus with a heartfelt request: 'Jesus, please rid my heart, soul, and mind of all fears, real or imaginary.' I could make a collection of those fears. Fear of death, darkness, dogs, flying, water, thunder, traffic, etc. There is no end to that list. We have all sorts of big words for abnormal fears of heights, of open spaces, of enclosed spaces, of water, etc. 'Fear doth make cowards of us all.' Fear can play such a large part in our lives that we owe it to ourselves, and to the quality of our lives, to get rid of that fear if at all possible.

What I want to say in this answer is that, of course, it is possible to be free from all fear. The father of John the Baptist greeted his birth with the song of gratitude for the good news that was about to be proclaimed: 'That, free from fear, and saved from the hands of our foes, we might serve the Lord in holiness and justice all the days of our lives in his presence.'

Yes, Jesus came to remove all fear. Again and again he told his apostles to 'Fear not'. 'Oh, why did you doubt, oh you of little faith?' When their boat was being tossed about on the high seas, in the midst of the storm, it is reasonable that the apostles should be afraid. Even then, however, Jesus was reminding them that, because he was with them, they should not be afraid. He told them that he would not abandon them, or leave them in the storm. He showed that he had power over all those things that caused them to fear, and he asked them to trust him to do that. On another occasion, the apostles were on their own in the boat, when a storm blew up, but Jesus came to them, walking on the water, and all was well. He went to great lengths to reinforce this fact, and he showed that he was serious in his advice to 'Be not afraid.'

Pope John Paul II wrote a masterpiece called *Crossing the Threshold of Hope*. This book has an interesting history. Plans were laid for a television personality to interview the Pope on many issues, and it was intended to give this interview a world-wide viewing. Pope John Paul was supplied with a list of questions that would form the nucleus of the interview. As it happened, however, the Pope was so busy that the plans fell through. Sometime later, however, the Pope contacted the person involved to tell him that he (Pope) had written out the answers to the questions, and he was willing to have those answers published in a book. The book was published shortly after that, and it became a bestseller.

The theme of the book could be summarised as 'Fear not; be not afraid'. These words are used again and again throughout the book. I have already quoted words from the homily of Pope Benedict, in his Mass in the Sistine Chapel with the cardinals the day after his election. However, his words are so important that I am going to quote him again, together with other words he spoke around that time. He told of his feelings at that time: 'On the one hand, a sense of inadequacy and human turmoil for the responsibility entrusted to me yesterday as the Successor of the Apostle Peter in the See of Rome, with regard to the Universal Church. On the other hand, I sense within me profound gratitude to God who does not abandon his flock, but leads it throughout time, under the guidance of those whom he has chosen as Vicars of his Son. This intimate recognition for a gift of divine mercy prevails in my heart in spite of everything. I consider this a grace obtained for me by my venerated predecessor, John Paul II. It seems I can feel his strong hand squeezing mine; I seem to see his smiling eyes, and listen to his words, addressed to me especially at this moment: "Do not be afraid".'

I quoted that homily at some length, because I believe that it highlights something that both of these wonderful men had grasped fully. Pope Benedict had learned well from his predecessor who, as he began his pontificate, had used the words, 'Do not be afraid! Open wide the doors for Christ!' I would like to quote Pope Benedict yet again, as he spoke during his inauguration Mass: 'Are we not perhaps all afraid in some way? If we let Christ enter fully into our lives, if we open ourselves totally to him, are we not afraid that he might take something away from us? Are we not perhaps afraid to give up something significant, something unique, something that makes life so beautiful? No! If we let Christ into our lives, we lose nothing, nothing, absolutely nothing of what makes life free, beautiful and great … Do not be afraid of Christ!'

Jesus called his Spirit 'The Comforter who would never leave us'. It was his intention that the Spirit should accompany us in all our endeavours. He does not want us ever to be alone, or to feel alone. When we live and walk in the Spirit, we have no reason to fear. All fear melts away before the power of God's Spirit. St John tells us, 'Little children, there is a Spirit within you that is greater than any evil spirit you will meet on the road of life.' After his anointing in the Jordan, Jesus was ready to take on all the evil that Satan might throw at him. He sent us his Spirit, so that we might have what he had, as we follow him all the way back into eternal life.

Part of being afraid is fear of the outcome, fear of what will happen to us. Jesus guarantees us the outcome of our lives, and this guarantee holds good for every step of that journey. Like a good shepherd, he will never abandon his flock. Jesus felt pity for the crowds that followed him because, in his words, they were like 'sheep without a shepherd'. To his listeners that was a very helpless situation to be in, and Jesus saw it in that way. When he asks us to follow him, he will never lead us where his Spirit and his grace will not be there to guide and protect us. With his call comes the grace to answer that call. An important part of our trust in him is that we can follow him without fear. His words 'Fear not. Be not afraid' apply especially to us when we are his disciples, and are following him. It is central to the guarantee that goes with the call. Our response to his call is made on trust. 'Oh why did you fear, you of little faith?' He could have said, 'Do you think I have called you so that I can abandon you, and leave all alone? I need your trust and your faith, so that you can step out in confidence, knowing that you will never be abandoned.'

The more I examine this counsel to 'Be not afraid', the more I realise that it has to do with taking Jesus at his word, and trusting his promises. St Padre Pio walked the road to Calvary, and it was only his trust in the promises of Jesus that enabled him do this. He was attacked by Satan, he was 'silenced' by superiors, he was maligned by his enemies, but nothing could destroy his profound confidence in the promises of Jesus. As he shares in eternal glory now, he would be very insistent to all of us that we need never have the slightest doubt, and we have no real reason to fear. Pope John Paul II lived his life out to the end, and accepted every suffering and limitation that came his way towards the end. I heard people criticise him for not retiring towards the end of his life, but he knew better. Even if he had to drag himself to that window and wave a hand, because he no longer had a voice, he continued to walk the walk, with deep confidence that all would be well. He probably touched more people during those final months than he did in his life up till then. His dying was as much a Christian witness as his living, and the whole world was gathered around his death-bed. If his voice allowed it, I am sure that he would have still exhorted us to 'Be not afraid.'

The question posed here is 'How is it possible to "Be Not Afraid"?' Even the question implies that it is possible. In the answer, I have tried to show that it is only possible when we walk with Jesus, in the power of his Spirit. It is not possible in any other way. Part of my willingness to follow Jesus must surely confront me with all of my fears.

Later on, this very day, I begin a weekend Retreat that involves healing services of many kinds. There will be services and anointings for the healing of memories, for the family tree, for relationships, for guilt and unforgiveness, but I hope to begin with a service of healing for fears of every kind. I expect this to be effective, because I know that Jesus wants me to proclaim his word boldly 'Be not afraid', and I also know that he is more than willing and ready to remove our fears, so that we can follow him with renewed trust and confidence. Reawakening our belief in his constant presence will greatly help to allay our fears.

When I was quite young, I would never have gone to a doctor or dentist unless my mother came with me. My mother was there for my first day in school, and she accompanied me on the day I went to boarding school. The first instinct of every child, when scared, is to run to the mother and find security and safety in her embrace. Mary my Mother says, 'Do whatever he tells you', because she knows only too well that he will never tell us, or ask us, to do something that would harm us in any way. We are children of God, and God is truly committed to take good care of all of his children, and we can trust him totally to do just that.

What is the secret of a happy life?

Anybody who has read the answers to the other questions in this book could make a good shot at answering this question, and of knowing already what I am likely to say! Obviously, *the* secret of a happy (and worthwhile) life is to 'live and to walk' in the Spirit. There could be nothing more effective for good than to live my life with the power of God.

Life is a journey, and God is offering to travel that journey with me. 'The Spirit will never leave you', is the promise of Jesus. All life comes from God. That I should exist, and be alive on the earth right now, is the result of a decision of God. In other words, he knows that I'm here! He is constantly and continuously aware of my existence, and of everything that happens to me. The Father is watching over me, Jesus is walking with me, and the Spirit is providing the inner life of my soul.

In God's eyes I am always a child, no matter what age my body may be. The secret of living happily is to plug into all the endless resources of life and love that are available in God. 'There is nothing impossible for God.' Never set limits to what God can do in your life because, if you do, God cannot work outside of those limits.

Most of us are probably 'cradle Christians'. We inherited our religion, and, during the earlier part of our lives we had very little personal input into what that involved. We were baptised before we knew a thing about what was happening around us. We were marched off to our First Confession (and probably given a list of 'sins', in case we forgot!). We processed up to our First Communion, and the same procedure accompanied our Confirmation. We were spoon-fed (force-fed?) pages and pages of catechism answers to questions, most of which we weren't asking, and probably still wouldn't think of asking most of them. Sooner or later, at some time or other (hopefully) the whole process will have ground to a halt. We'll have come to a point in our lives where we ask, 'What's it all about, Alfie?' Now we will have plenty of questions, but they will be ours. 'The greatest problem with religion are not the questions of the atheist for which there are no answers, but the answers of the catechist for which there were no questions'! If we are really blessed, we will have met some person of God who will help guide us towards the answers. Note that I'm not hoping for someone who knows all the answers! All I ask for is someone who is anointed with God's Spirit, and everything will be well. We will have discovered the fountain of living water, and our lives will be transformed.

Unfortunately, for many people, this encounter does not happen until they have travelled through barren deserts, taken many a wrong road, ended up in cul-de-sacs, and were forced to fall on their knees. It is not possible for a person to fall on his knees, cry out to God, and not be heard. We may not be broken, but it's ok to be slightly cracked! The Spirit enters our hearts through the cracks. If I have not discovered my human weakness and powerlessness, then I'm not very likely to be open to Good News about forgiveness, redemption, salvation, or a Higher Power.

It is said that 'prevention is better than cure', which is true but, unfortunately, many of us have to come to the Lord with our broken toys and shattered dreams, and allow him create us all over again. This is called 'being born again'. Salvation is the grace I get to start again at any moment of my life. Life involves the repetition of a constant 'Yes' to God, and the only 'Yes' God is ever interested in is our 'Yes' of now.

We have so much to learn from our Mother Mary. She didn't actually do anything herself. Rather she gave God permission to do whatever he wanted with her. She surrendered to God as a servant (handmaid), and she just accepted, without questioning everything that happened after that. She questioned the Archangel, and she questioned Jesus when she found him in the Temple. After that there were no more questions. She just believed that God knew best, that he knew what he was doing, and why, and hers was just to obey and trust. In surrendering to God, she had handed her will and her life over to him, and she was like Jesus who said that he came, not to do his own will, but the will of him who sent him.

This kind of spirituality is quite a paradox. Life encourages us to succeed, to overcome, to achieve. It is faulty merchandise, however, because earthly success is very fragile, and the rust and the moth can destroy it. The gospels tell us that if we surrender to a Higher Power, if we just open our hands and let go of the clammy coins, that we will be blessed enormously and abundantly. 'It is in giving that we receive, and in dying that we're born to eternal life.' This is pure gold success that can never corrupt or decay. This is happiness that the world can never give. This is investing in the Bank of Heaven, where the dividends are unending.

Another important ingredient for a happy life is *gratitude*. It is not possible to be grateful and unhappy at the same time. If I am open to God's love, my heart will constantly sing songs of joy and gratitude. Gratitude is very refreshing for the spirit, and the grateful soul is always fully alive. Jesus said that he came that we 'might have life, and have it in abundance'. If we have abundant life, then our hearts will overflow with gratitude. That gratitude, firstly, will be poured out on those around me. 'If you say you love God, whom you cannot see, and hate your brother, whom you do see, you are a liar, and the truth is not in you', says St John. God doesn't want to hear me saying 'thanks' to him, unless those around me hear it first. 'How sharper than a serpent's tooth it is to have a thankless child', lamented King Lear about his daughters. To be grateful is to be gracious, and this is directly connected with the word 'grace'.

It is a blessing to encounter a person who appreciates the goodness of others. It is very confirming for any of us who receives gratitude and appreciation from others. Dimus Shacherian, the founder of *The Full Gospel Fellowship*, wrote a book called *The Happiest People on Earth*. No guessing who those people are! No, not the millionaires, or those who dwell in mansions on Sunset

Boulevard! The happiness that is spoken of in this book is the happiness that comes from serving others. These are the people that Jesus calls 'Blessed' in the Eight Beatitudes. Those who are grateful are grateful for what they have, and don't pine after more and more of this world's goods, or its acclaim. 'What do you give someone who has everything?' Goldwater, the billionaire, was asked. 'More' came the immediate reply. There is not enough money in the world to make some people happy, just as there's never enough alcohol for the alcoholic. 'Not on bread alone do people live, but on every word that comes out of the mouth of God.' How true a statement that is! There is a hunger and thirst within the human spirit that can never be satisfied with the goods of this world.

One of the tragedies in this world are the countless millions who have been displaced by famine or war. Their greatest poverty is that they do not belong. Belonging is a very necessary security for any of us. We belong to a family, a Christian community, a workforce, a nation, or a sports club. To have a sense of belonging is a necessary requisite for contentment. The first victims of war and aggression are the poor, who are displaced, and become refugees, while the 'powers' of this world satisfy their lust for control and conquest. Most of us take it for granted to belong to a family, and to have a house which is a home. We may have secure employment, and a comfortable lifestyle. This is certainly not a problem, unless, of course, we take it for granted and fail to appreciate the blessings that are ours.

There are people, however, who can have what is needed for a contented life, but who never really get involved in life around them. This is evident at the level of the parish, where the same people are saddled with all the ministries and services, because others refuse to become involved. Being a member of a Christian community implies involvement, and we all have a role to play in the life of the community. Not to give is to miss out on the receiving. We know of people who have a 'lazy eye', a withered hand, or a useless leg. This image could well apply to the Body of Christ, which is the parish. The Christian must always hear the call to serve. Everyone of us can contribute something. The person who gives is the one who receives, and one can feel sorry, indeed, for those people who miss out on so much by not being involved. We are all familiar with Scrooge who, while he hoarded and would not share, was miserable to himself and to others. Once he began to give, he was totally transformed. The deeper my sense of belonging, the better my quality of life.

I have dealt with one of the core secrets of a happy life, when I answered the question about living in the 'now'. Not to live in the 'now' can cause intense mental strain, when part of me is trying to relive yesterday, and the rest of me is planning tomorrow. Because yesterday no longer exists, and tomorrow does not exist yet, I am living in some sort of 'no-man's time', if not in a 'no-man's land'.

The secret of a happy life is to live life fully. Living is so much more than merely existing. Today is a very different day from yesterday. God is a God of surprises, and co-incidents are often God's way of preserving his anonymity! Allow yourself to be surprised by God by being aware of his presence and his action in your life. Don't settle for drifting or day-dreaming. Stretch out the antennae as far as possible, and be aware of what's going on around you.

Life is always happening. Life is what's happening when you're making other plans. Life is given to be lived, and we are called to become fully human and fully alive. There is a need to be as down-to-earth as I can, which is another way of living in reality. I have a friend, recovering from alcoholism, who returned to the bottle because he found reality too painful. In his case, it was a short-term pain that would have produced a long-term gain, but he didn't have the will to continue with it. After years of nicotine, alcohol, etc., a person gets used to reaching for the anaesthetic, for the 'fix', or the quick solution. 'Happy are they who dream dreams and are prepared to pay the price to make those dreams come true' (Cardinal Suenens).

I like to speak about 'getting stuck into life', immersing myself fully in the process, and using my time well. Life is full of opportunities and, if missed, they may never come back again. We sin 'in what we do, and in what we fail to do.' 'Sins of omission' could rank among my greatest and most frequent.

Earlier in this answer I spoke about the importance of *gratitude* as a secret of a happy life. I mentioned being grateful to those around me, and now I would like to make a few comments on being grateful to God. Jesus was hurt when only one of the ten lepers returned to thank him for their healing. He was probably sorry for them that they should be so ungrateful. Prayer comes naturally to the grateful heart. My heart can be singing a song of thanks, without my lips saying a word. 'Rejoice in the Lord always, again I say rejoice.' There are many instances in the gospels where Jesus began his prayer by giving thanks to the Father. 'Father, I thank you that you have hidden these things from the clever and the worldly-wise, and revealed them to mere children.' For the miracle of the loaves and fish, and at the Last Supper 'Jesus took the bread, gave thanks …' Before calling Lazarus forth from the tomb, he prayed, 'Father, I thank you that have already heard me …' People who have the Spirit within them are always truly grateful. No wonder Mary sang her *Magnificat*, because the Lord had done so much for her, and holy is his name. As I said, prayer comes naturally to the grateful heart.

There are many other ingredients of a happy life, but I will deal with just one more. That one is *truth*. In a way, I suppose, we are speaking about the Spirit here again, whom Jesus called 'the Spirit of truth'. A very important word is, 'The Spirit will bring you into all truth, and the truth will set you free.' The liar has to have a good memory! Those involved in lies and deceit can really mess up their lives and, indeed, greatly damage the lives of those around them. I do not believe that a deceitful person can be a happy person. In a way, such a person is always 'on the run', continually looking over his shoulder, waiting for someone to catch him out in his web of lies. Such a person could not be happy.

Instead of continuing down through a list of 'goods' and

'bads', I return to where I began in this answer. If I learn to live and to walk in the Spirit, then gratitude, honesty, prayer, etc., will be part of my very everyday living. Only God is constant. The shortest distance between two points is a straight line. God is a straight line, constant, ever present, and always reliable. On the other hand, we, as humans, are like a graph, rising one day and dipping the next. It is only God who can provide any constancy and consistency to our lives. 'Jesus is the same yesterday, today, and always.' My life is what I make it, in so far as the decisions are under my control. God is on 'stand-by', waiting to enter wherever he is invited. Maranatha! Come Lord Jesus!